Reservist's Money Guide

RESERVIST'S MONEY GUIDE

1st Edition

P. J. Budahn

STACKPOLE
BOOKS

Published by
STACKPOLE BOOKS
5067 Ritter Road
Mechanicsburg, PA 17055

This book is not an official publication of the Department of Defense, nor does its publication in any way imply its endorsement by this agency.

Cover design by Wendy Reynolds

Printed in the United States of America

10 9 8 7 6 5 4 3 2 1

First Edition

Library of Congress Cataloging-in-Publication Data

Budahn, P. J. (Phillip J.), 1949–
Reservists' money guide / P. J. Budahn.—1st ed.
p. cm.
Includes index.
ISBN 0-8117-2917-6
1. United States—Armed Forces—Reserves—Pay, allowances, etc. 2. Consumer education. I. Title
UC80.B84 1997
335.3'7'0973—dc21 97-22437
CIP

CONTENTS

PREFACE

A funny thing happened to the U.S. military on the way to the post–Cold War drawdown. The armed forces ended up with more "weekend warriors" than full-time, active-duty people.

Always an important contributor to the nation's wartime force, the men and women of the reserves and National Guard are increasingly being called away from their homes and families to deal with global hot spots.

Reservist's Money Guide is designed to help them make sense of a bewildering array of programs, benefits, and payments that have a direct impact on their financial well-being.

The language is simple, jargon-free English. The organization is straightforward. Who gets what? Is it taxable? What are the typical glitches affecting eligibility? Can it be earned for weekend drill periods or two-week summer training camps?

Our focus is on the men and women of all of the reserve components—Army Reserves, Naval Reserves, Air Force Reserves, Marine Corp Reserves, Coast Guard Reserves, Army National Guard, and Air National Guard—plus their families.

You shouldn't have to be a military veteran to understand military benefits. For that reason, *Reservist's Money Guide* is proud to bear the label "spouse-friendly."

My thanks go to the real experts in reserve affairs and personnel issues, who helped assemble the information in this volume. The men and women who administer the military's personnel programs, along with their counterparts in the Department of Veterans Affairs, are the unrecognized jewels of the federal sector. Any errors are mine.

Whenever you are about to confront the jumbled network of regulations, rules, and procedures surrounding the military's personnel policies, it's useful to remember that each one was put in place by Congress or the Pentagon to solve a particular problem.

Sometimes the execution is faulty, sometimes the problem has been solved but the program lingers on, and sometimes bad information about the fine print is endlessly perpetuated.

The payments and programs for the reserve components were created by a grateful nation to help its citizen-soldiers. *Reservist's Money Guide* is a tool to ensure that you—and your loved ones—have the information you need, in language you can understand, and in a format that makes sense.

PART I

PAY FUNDAMENTALS

1

BASIC PAY

In This Chapter:

- *Eligibility*
- *Rates*
- *Taxes*

Basic Pay is the closest thing that the military has to a salary. With a few notable exceptions, everyone on active duty gets Basic Pay. It is unaffected by job, location of assignment, other military bonuses, or outside income.

For reservists and those in the National Guard, there may be some uncertainty about exactly who—or, more precisely, what kind of duty—qualifies for Basic Pay. Here are the fundamentals.

ELIGIBILITY

Reservists and National Guardsmen who are formally classified as being on active duty are eligible to receive Basic Pay. This includes people whose formal military status is:

- Extended active duty
- Full-time training duty
- Active-duty training
- Active duty for training

- Annual training duty
- Attendance at service school
- Temporary active duty

The first two categories—extended active duty and full-time training duty—consist of reservists and guard members on full-time military service.

The other categories include members of the reserve components who are on active duty for short fixed periods, such as the fourteen or fifteen days of the typical summer training period for most reserve and National Guard units.

For reservists, Basic Pay begins when they leave home for the active-duty assignment, and it ends when they return home.

For National Guardsmen ordered to active duty for less than thirty days, Basic Pay begins when they appear at unit assembly areas, usually the nearest National Guard Armory, not when they leave home. For longer periods, it begins when they leave home.

Basic Pay is paid for full days. A day's Basic Pay is never divided to reflect the actual number of hours on active duty.

Here's how the eligibility rules for Basic Pay affect reservists and National Guardsmen in specific situations:

Active Duty without Pay: Reservists and guardsmen may be brought on active duty without Basic Pay, but only with their consent.

Some people may be asked by the military to serve on active duty "without allowances." This means without the Basic Allowance for Quarters (BAQ), the Basic Allowance for Subsistence (BAS), and some other kinds of pay.

Advance Pay: When reservists and guardsmen are called to active duty for at least 140 days, they can receive one month's Basic Pay in advance. Usually, approval is automatic for a one-month advance.

An advance of up to three months' Basic Pay can be made

with a commander's approval, and commanders have considerable discretion.

Advance payments must be repaid by deductions from military paychecks. Repayment must be made within a year or before the end of the active-duty period, whichever comes first.

Disability Compensation: Reserve members receiving Disability Compensation from the Department of Veterans Affairs (VA) cannot receive it and Basic Pay at the same time. They must give one up.

If they surrender VA Disability Compensation, they lose one-thirtieth of their monthly VA checks for each day on which they draw Basic Pay. If they surrender Basic Pay, they also lose every other kind of payment that goes into an active-duty paycheck.

Drill Pay: Reservists and guardsmen cannot receive Drill Pay (officially known as inactive-duty pay) for any calendar day for which they also receive Basic Pay. This is true even when they perform duties that would normally qualify them for Drill Pay on the first or last day of an active-duty stretch.

> No one can receive Basic Pay and Drill Pay for the same day.

Illness: Reserve-component members continue to receive Basic Pay if illness or injury prevents them from performing their military duties after they've reported for active duty.

Jail: People receiving Basic Pay lose it and the rest of their paychecks if they're confined by military or civilian law authorities.

Leave: Anyone who serves on active duty for at least 30 consecutive days is entitled to military leave. Leave is accumulated at the rate of 2.5 calendar days for each month.

There's no credit for leave days during active-duty periods of 29 days or less, unapproved absences, and confinement.

If the leave hasn't been used by the time the reservist leaves active duty, it can be cashed in. Military members receive one-thirtieth of monthly Basic Pay for each cashed-in leave day. No other kinds of military compensation—such as BAQ, BAS or special pays—are counted when leave is cashed in.

National Guard: Basic Pay goes only to members of the National Guard who are on active duty for the federal government. It doesn't go to those who are on active duty for their states.

Physicals: Basic Pay begins for some reservists and members of the National Guard as soon as they report for a pre-call-up physical examination. This applies only to people scheduled to be on active duty for thirty days or more.

Physical examinations not followed by active-duty time don't qualify for Basic Pay.

Retired Pay: Reserve-component members receiving military retired pay cannot receive it and Basic Pay at the same time. They must give one up. If they surrender Basic Pay, they also lose every other category of pay that goes into an active-duty paycheck.

Travel: Reservists and National Guard members are entitled to Basic Pay while traveling to their active-duty locations. National Guardsmen receive Basic Pay while traveling from the hometown unit assembly areas to the active-duty site.

Within the forty-eight contiguous states, all reserve-component members usually receive one extra day's Basic Pay at the beginning of that active-duty stint and another day's Basic Pay when they return home at the end. These two extra days of Basic Pay also go to reserve-component members traveling to an active-duty station by air.

Reserve-component members can be credited with more days of basic pay when they are authorized to drive from their homes to the active-duty site. Reservists and guardsmen who drive at least 526 miles between home and the assignment are credited with at least two day's Basic Pay for the incoming drive and at least another two days for the return trip.

RATES

Reservists and National Guardsmen who are eligible for Basic Pay receive the same rates as full-time active-duty service members. Amounts are based solely on rank and years of service.

For 1997, rates range from $833.40 a month for a new recruit to $9,016.80 a month for a four-star general or admiral.

Members of the reserve components who are on active duty for less than thirty days receive the daily rate of Basic Pay, which is determined by dividing monthly Basic Pay by thirty.

Those spending more than thirty days on active duty will receive the daily rate (one-thirtieth of the monthly rate) for each day of the first and last months on active duty.

The amount of Basic Pay isn't decreased when military members receive any other compensation from the armed forces, although reservists and guard members are ineligible to receive Drill Pay, retired pay, or VA disability compensation for any day they're paid Basic Pay.

Recipients of Basic Pay can direct the finance center to send some of their pay directly to other people, a process called allotments.

Basic Pay is also subject to the legal process called garnishment, in which a court directs the military to divert money from a military paycheck to settle debts or other obligations.

Here are some other fine points affecting Basic Pay rates for members of the reserves and National Guard on active duty:

Rank: For those having dual status—both an active-duty and a reserve rank—Basic Pay is paid at the rank mentioned in the call-up orders. Generally, that is the reserve rank, except for those on extended active duty.

Some services and units permit people who've been

approved for promotion to wear their new, higher rank before the official promotion date. This is called "frocking." Regardless of what rank you're wearing on your uniform, Basic Pay is the older, lower rate until the promotion is official.

Years of Service: Time in the reserves and National Guard is used to compute the years-of-service portion of the Basic Pay chart.

The years-of-service figure isn't linked to actual participation in reserve activities, payment for inactive duty, or earning "points" toward retirement.

However, for the reserve time to count, a person must formally be a member of the reserves or National Guard. For an example, an E-5 who spent four years on active duty and three years in the reserves receives the same Basic Pay as an E-5 with seven continuous years on active duty.

The clock on years of service stops whenever a reservist or guard member is discharged from the reserve component and fails to reenlist immediately.

Also not counted toward the years-of-service requirement is time spent in the inactive National Guard; absent without leave from the reserves, National Guard, or active duty; or without any reserve or National Guard obligation.

TAXES

With one notable exception, Basic Pay is fully taxable. It is subject to federal income taxes, Social Security taxes, Medicare taxes, and state income taxes.

Like other taxpayers, servicemembers can direct their employer—in this case, the U.S. government—to withhold enough money from each paycheck to take care of their federal and state income tax liability. Forms are available at unit finances offices.

The exception to the taxability rule is called the "combat-zone exclusion." Military members serving in an officially designated combat zone get a tax break. This is fully discussed in Chapter 6.

2

DRILL PAY

In This Chapter:

- *Eligibility*
- *Rates*
- *Adjustments*
- *Financial Protection*
- *Excluded Benefits*
- *Muster Pay*

What sets members of the reserve components apart from their full-time brethren is that some of their most valuable contributions to the nation come during weekend drill periods and two-week stints of active-duty training.

For these periods, which are officially classified as inactive duty, the Pentagon and Congress have tailored the military's pay system to meet the needs of both the part-time soldiers and the services.

ELIGIBILITY

All reservists and members of the National Guard can qualify to receive Drill Pay, which is officially known as inactive-duty pay.

Whether a particular individual actually receives Drill Pay depends on two things. One is the person's membership in a part of the reserve component. The other involves the type of duty performed by that reservist or guardsman.

First, to be eligible, a Drill Pay recipient must officially be a member of one of the following:

- Air Force Reserve
- Air Force of the U.S.
- Air National Guard
- Air National Guard of the U.S.
- Army of the U.S.
- Army National Guard
- Army National Guard of the U.S.
- Army Reserve
- Coast Guard Reserve (includes temporary members)
- Marine Corps Reserve
- National Guard
- National Guard of the U.S.
- Naval Reserve
- Nurse Corps Reserve of Public Health Service
- Reserve Corps of Public Health Service

Second, Drill Pay recipients must perform duties or undergo training for which a unit or parent service has authorized the extra money. Commonly, Drill Pay recipients are paid for:

- Inactive-duty training
- Unit training assembly (UTA)
- Additional flying training period (AFTP)
- Additional inactive-duty training
- Other equivalent training, instruction, or duty

Whatever the category, reservists and guardsmen must serve for at least two hours during a single day to qualify for Drill Pay.

If commanders have approved in advance a fixed period of duty or training for Drill Pay, reservists cannot qualify for more money by exceeding the authorized time limit.

Here's how the rules governing Drill Pay apply in specific circumstances:

Advance Pay: There are no provisions for reservists and

guard members to receive advance payments of Drill Pay. Money is paid as it's earned.

Basic Pay: A military member cannot receive Basic Pay and Drill Pay for the same calendar day, even though a servicemember may spend a portion of a calendar day on active duty and a portion on inactive duty.

Typically, members of the reserve components who qualify for both Basic Pay and Drill Pay for the same day surrender the Drill Pay, because they have written orders requiring them to be on active duty that day.

Disability Compensation: Reserve component members receiving VA Disability Compensation cannot receive it and Drill Pay at the same time. They must give one up.

If they surrender VA Disability Compensation, they lose one-thirtieth of their monthly VA checks for each official drill period that they draw Drill Pay. Since the typical training day consists of two drill periods, most recipients of VA Disability Compensation would lose two-thirtieths of their monthly VA checks for each calendar day for which they received Drill Pay.

If they surrender Drill Pay, they also lose every other pay category that goes into their paychecks as members of the reserve components.

Inactive Duty without Pay: Reservists and guard members may take part in unit training or individual training without receiving Drill Pay, with their consent. Frequently, this happens when members are trying to amass points for retirement. They can receive points for periods when they're not given Drill Pay.

Leave: People drawing Drill Pay don't accumulate any credit toward military leave.

Muster Pay: Members of the reserve components cannot receive Drill Pay for any calendar day for which they're also authorized Muster Pay, even if they perform duties or training for which they would normally receive Drill Pay. The rules don't allow people to give up Muster Pay in order to collect Drill Pay.

National Guard: Drill Pay goes only to members of the National Guard who are undergoing training for the federal government. It doesn't go to those who are performing training on behalf of their states.

Other Pays: In addition to Drill Pay, reservists and National Guard members are eligible for certain other kinds of military pay during weekend drills and other periods of inactive duty.

Eligibility isn't automatic. Servicemembers must meet the eligibility rules for any additions to the military paycheck, including:

- Affiliation Bonus
- Demolition Pay
- Diving Pay
- Enlisted Flight Pay
- Enlistment Bonuses
- Experimental Stress Pay
- Flight Deck Pay
- Flight Pay (ACIP)
- Foreign Duty Pay
- Foreign Language Pay
- Initial Clothing Allowance (women only)
- Maternity Clothing Allowance
- Medical and Nurses' Sign-up Bonuses
- Parachute Pay
- Reenlistment Bonuses
- Sea Pay
- Special Duty Assignment Pay
- Submarine Pay

Details about these paycheck additions can be found in the appropriate chapters of *Reservist's Money Guide*.

Retirees: Military retirees can belong to the reserve components but they cannot receive retired pay and Drill Pay for the same calendar day. They must give one up.

If they surrender their retired pay, they lose one-thirtieth of their monthly retirement checks for each calendar day for which they draw Drill Pay. Note that this system matches one day of retired pay with one day of Drill Pay.

If military retirees surrender Drill Pay, they also lose every other pay category that goes into their paychecks as members of the reserve component.

Travel: Recipients of Drill Pay are usually ineligible for military travel benefits when going to or from their units. There are two exceptions:

First, reserve component members can be reimbursed for travel-related expenses incurred while performing official business for their units while drawing Drill Pay.

Second, reservists and guard members drawing Drill Pay and sent for training or duties at locations other than their regular units can qualify for some travel benefits.

RATES

Payment for one drill period equals one-thirtieth of the monthly Basic Pay appropriate for the rank and years-of-service category of each reservist and guardsman.

A drill period is seldom a calendar day. By regulation, it must be at least two hours long. Frequently, it's four hours.

This means that a typical reservist or guard member performing a typical two-day weekend drill assignment is credited with four drill periods and earns four-thirtieths of one month's Basic Pay.

Regardless of the actual time spent in training, reservists and guardsmen cannot be paid for more than two drill periods in one calendar day.

Drill Pay automatically increases when Congress approves a change in Basic Pay for active-duty servicemembers.

When reservists and guard members are promoted, they become eligible for Drill Pay at the new, higher rank for the

In 1920, Congress first defined Drill Pay as one-thirtieth the monthly rate for Basic Pay.

first drill period after the effective date of the promotion, as noted on their orders. When the official promotion date is also a drill day, Drill Pay is paid at the new, higher rate for that day.

ADJUSTMENTS

Drill Pay may be small in comparison to an active-duty paycheck, but reservists and guardsmen have the same financial responsibilities as full-time servicemembers.

A variety of factors can affect—usually by decreasing—the amount of money that actually shows up in a paycheck for Drill Pay. Here are some of the major adjustments to Drill Pay:

Allotments: An allotment is an instruction given by a military member to the finance center to send a portion of his paycheck directly to another person or agency.

Usually, Drill Pay and other payments to reservists and guardsmen who are officially on inactive-duty status cannot be broken down into allotments. There are two major exceptions:

- National Guard members purchasing state-sponsored life insurance
- Premiums for federally sponsored life insurance

Article 15s: Reservists and National Guardsmen who are drawing Drill Pay are subject to the military's basic law, the Uniform Code of Military Justice (UCMJ). That includes the UCMJ's provisions for so-called nonjudicial punishment, more commonly known as "Article 15s" or "Captain's Mast."

Members of the reserve component subject to Article 15s can have fines taken from the Drill Pay as well as from any active-duty pay they receive.

The authority of Article 15s applies to all reservists and

guard members, including reserve component members serving without pay to earn retirement points.

Court-martial: When military members are sentenced by courts-martial to fines and forfeitures of pay, Drill Pay can be reduced to satisfy those debts.

This applies to reservists and members of the National Guard sentenced to lose money during earlier tours on active duty, as well as to people sentenced to lose money during annual active-duty training periods.

These obligations continue—whether the reserve component member is drawing Drill Pay or Basic Pay—until the court-martial sentence has been fulfilled.

Reservists and guardsmen get two breaks when these sentences are applied to Drill Pay. First, most sentences have clear time limits. Take the case of a fine of $100 a month for ten months. What if the reservist's monthly Drill Pay doesn't equal $100? The servicemember would lose all Drill Pay for ten months but would be eligible for full Drill Pay in the eleventh month, even if the government hadn't received $1,000.

Second, percentages based on Basic Pay—not dollar amounts—are used for fines taken from Drill Pay. Consider a sentence of $100 forfeiture of Basic Pay for ten months, when the servicemember's Basic Pay is $1,000. The fine is for 10 percent of Basic Pay. In this example, the servicemember would have 10 percent of Drill Pay withheld for ten months.

Life Insurance: Reservists and guard members drawing Drill Pay are eligible to purchase Servicemembers' Group Life Insurance (SGLI). Like those on active duty, they must pay premiums for the coverage, which are deducted from their pay.

The minimum coverage is $100,000, which costs $8.50 a month. The maximum coverage is $200,000, which costs $17 a month.

Reservists and guardsmen who are members of the Individual Ready Reserve (IRR) and the Inactive National Guard

(ING) can also purchase SGLI coverage. Normally, these members of the reserve components don't receive Drill Pay. They pay their premiums by writing checks for the coverage.

Old Soldiers' Home: Drill Pay isn't subject to the automatic $1 monthly deduction from the paychecks of all active-duty servicemembers to offset expenses of the U.S. Soldiers' and Airmen's Home and the U.S. Naval Home.

Taxes: Drill Pay is fully taxable. It is subject to federal, state, Social Security, and Medicare taxes.

For communities that have a locality tax, which is essentially a community income tax, reservists and guardsmen who are residents of those communities have the locality tax drawn from Drill Pay if their drill periods are performed within their home states.

Tax withholding for locality taxes is voluntary when reservists and guardsmen serve on inactive-duty status outside their home states.

FINANCIAL PROTECTION

Even for part-time soldiers, military service can be dangerous. Threats to life, limb, employability, and the financial security of their families cannot be eliminated from all drill periods.

Other chapters of *Reservist's Money Guide* have complete details about financial protection for military members injured during drill periods. Included here is a quick summary of those programs.

> "Inactive-duty status" usually means actively participating with reserve units or undergoing training.

All the following programs affect everyone who's officially classified as performing inactive duty. Those with orders permitting them to earn points for retirement while not receiving any military pay are also qualified for these benefits.

Medical Care: Reservists and members of the National Guard who develop medical problems—injuries, illnesses, or diseases—during drill periods are entitled to free medical and dental care from the military.

This also applies to those folks who aggravate medical problems during drill periods. Additionally, it applies to members of the reserve components who are traveling to or from drill periods.

Ineligible are servicemembers whose medical problems are related to some misconduct, such as drinking or drug abuse.

This is a short-term benefit. Most permanently injured reservists and guardsmen are discharged, and responsibility for their continuing medical problems passes to the VA medical system, which is designed to provide free lifetime care.

VA Disability Pay: Reservists and guard members can receive monthly payments called VA Disability Compensation for permanent disabilities related to mishaps during drill periods.

> Military retirees and recipients of VA Disability Compensation cannot collect that money when they earn Drill Pay.

As with the rules for medical care, the health problems can be injuries, illnesses, or diseases that were incurred or aggravated during drill periods. The problems can also be related to events traveling to or from drill periods.

VA Disability Compensation is tax free. Amounts are based on the severity of a veteran's problem and are expressed as a percentage. In 1997, rates ranged from $94 a month for a 10 percent disability to $1,924 a month for a 100 percent disability.

These percentages are based on a rigorous medical screening, with VA officials following detailed guidelines. Percentages can increase if a veteran's health deteriorates.

Incapacitation Pay: It is possible to have a medical problem that isn't serious enough to qualify for VA Disability Compensation, even though it interferes with one's full-time civilian career.

Incapacitation Pay was developed for medical problems that were caused or aggravated by military service and that reduce total income.

The maximum rate is a combination of a servicemember's Basic Pay, Basic Allowance for Quarters (BAQ), and Basic Allowance for Subsistence (BAS). From these three kinds of pay is subtracted any other income that a reservist or guardsman receives, including sick leave or disability pay from a civilian employer.

Incapacitation Pay has a six-month limit. It ends sooner if the recipient recovers earlier. People who still have medical problems after six months can apply for—and should receive—VA Disability Compensation.

Survivor's Pension: A sad reality is that people can die while serving their country during weekend drill periods.

When a reserve-component member dies during a drill period, or when such a death occurs later but was clearly caused by an injury that happened while on drill status, the servicemember's spouse and children can qualify for a monthly payment from the government.

Called Dependency and Indemnity Compensation (DIC), it provides a monthly income for spouses. In 1997, the monthly rate was $833, with another $211 a month for each underaged child.

For DIC to be given, the connection between the servicemember's death and military service must be clear. A maze of rules applies when the connection isn't obvious.

EXCLUDED BENEFITS

Often, when trying to come to grips for the first time with the finer points of military pay policy, it's useful to get a clear understanding of what you're *not* eligible to receive.

This is especially true for members of the reserve components who are drawing Drill Pay or who volunteer to serve on inactive-duty status without pay to earn retirement points.

For them, some of the major additions to a military paycheck won't show up in their paychecks. Details on all these programs are located in the appropriate chapters of *Reservist's Money Guide*. Here are some of the high points:

Basic Pay: The rates for Drill Pay are based on rates for Basic Pay, but reservists and members of the National Guard cannot receive Basic Pay and Drill Pay for the same calendar day.

Basic Allowance for Quarters: Reservists and guardsmen are ineligible for BAQ based on drill periods, regardless of how many drill periods they perform in a row.

Basic Allowance for Subsistence: Members of the reserve components cannot receive BAS payments for service during drill periods or other stretches of inactive-duty status.

Medical Care: The only medical care authorized to reservists and National Guard members on inactive-duty status is treatment for medical problems that arise during drill periods. They're ineligible for treatment for health problems that aren't caused or aggravated by their service during drill periods.

Dependent Medical Care: The families—officially, the dependents—of reserve-component members are ineligible for military medical care while the servicemember is attending drill periods or even during the two-week annual stint on active duty for training.

Variable Housing Allowance (VHA): No VHA payments can be made to reservists and guardsmen until they're officially brought on active duty. Even then, members of the reserve components usually must be ordered onto active duty for at least twenty weeks to qualify for VHA.

Overseas Housing Allowance (OHA): Reservists and National Guard members who are on inactive-duty status are ineligible to receive OHA payments.

CONUS (or Stateside) Cost-of-Living-Adjustment (COLA): Members of the reserve components must be ordered to active duty for at least twenty weeks to be eligible for the new income supplement for servicemembers living in high-cost stateside areas.

MUSTER PAY

Another payment is on the books for reservists that, in many respects, resembles Drill Pay. Called Muster Pay, it goes to members of the reserves who are ordered by their parent service to perform specific tasks in an inactive-duty status.

Eligibility: Muster Pay is paid to reservists who've been ordered to report to a reserve center for a one-day examination of their records and a quick physical.

Ineligible for this extra payment are any National Guard members, members of drilling reserve units, and members of the Individual Mobilization Augmentation (IMA) program.

People recalled for muster duty must be present at least two hours at their assigned locations to qualify. They are ineligible for Basic Pay, any other active-duty-related pay, Drill Pay, or any other inactive-duty-related pay for a calendar day during which they receive Muster Pay.

Muster Pay can be paid only once a year to an individual.

Rates: Everyone receives the same amount of Muster Pay. Rank, time in service, and time in grade have no bearing. The amount, which varies slightly from year to year, was $124 in 1997.

From that is subtracted federal and state income tax and 50 cents for SGLI. No Social Security taxes are withheld from Muster Pay.

Under federal law, payment of Muster Pay must be made on or before the day of the muster.

A day for which one receives Muster Pay doesn't count toward computing reserve retirements.

3

Basic Allowance for Quarters

In This Chapter:

- *Eligibility*
- *Overview on Rates*
- *The With-Dependents Rate*
- *The Partial Rate*
- *Taxes*
- *Dual-Service Couples*
- *Special Circumstances*

People on active duty are entitled to government housing. If the government doesn't provide a roof over their heads, it provides some additional cash in the monthly paycheck in the form of Basic Allowance for Quarters (BAQ).

Reservists and members of the National Guard can qualify for BAQ payments, although that usually happens only when a servicemember is on full-time military duty.

ELIGIBILITY

BAQ can be paid to any member of the reserve component who is officially listed as being on active duty.

The length of time on active duty doesn't affect eligibility, nor does the length of time mentioned on the original orders or the length of time that the parent service originally intended to keep the reservist or guardsman on active duty.

BAQ Summary

Purpose:	To pay for off-base housing
Amounts:	$202.50 to $1,015.20 a month (1997)
Rates:	By rank, dependents
Taxable:	No
Loopholes:	Not affected by actual housing expenses
Problem areas:	Not applicable to drill periods; complexities involving divorce or separation when children are involved.

Ineligible are reservists and guard members who aren't on active duty. This includes reserve-component members technically classified as being on inactive-duty status, which applies to recipients of Drill Pay and people who are earning points for retirement by unpaid duties and training.

Two broad factors affect an individual's eligibility: active-duty status and housing situation. A third factor affecting eligibility is call-up for "contingency operations." Guardsmen have some distinct concerns when it comes to BAQ eligibility.

Status: BAQ is linked to Basic Pay. Everyone receiving Basic Pay has passed the first eligibility hurdle. This includes people who formally fall into one of the following categories:

- Extended active duty
- Full-time training duty
- Active-duty training
- Active duty for training
- Annual training duty
- Attendance at service school
- Temporary active duty

Eligibility for BAQ is always for full days. One day's BAQ is never divided to reflect the actual number of hours on active duty or to reflect any other portion of a day.

Housing: Usually, you should get BAQ if you aren't given government family housing. Conversely, if you are provided with government housing for your dependents, you usually don't get BAQ.

Most members of the reserve components aren't offered on-base housing for their families during short active-duty stints for training. This means that they typically qualify for BAQ.

Reservists and guard members on extended active duty, full-time training duty, or any other kind of active duty in which their full-time job is military service can find themselves assigned to military family housing under the same rules that apply to the rest of the active-duty force.

Contingency: Most military people without family members who officially qualify as dependents lose BAQ payments when the government provides housing for them.

Members of the reserve components get a break. Those without official dependents can receive BAQ at the appropriate without-dependents rate under a specific set of circumstances. Servicemembers must be:

- Brought on active duty in support of a contingency operation.
- Unable to continue to occupy the homes where they lived before the call-up.
- Legally obligated to maintain those homes, under either a rental agreement or a mortgage.

An example of a contingency operation would be a near-wartime situation such as Desert Shield, the buildup to Desert Storm.

Reservists and National Guard members lose this special protection if their call-up orders authorize transportation of their household goods to their new assignments.

OVERVIEW ON RATES

BAQ rates are unaffected by the actual costs of off-base housing. If you spend less for rent or a mortgage than you receive in BAQ, you can keep the difference. However, if your lodging costs exceed your BAQ payment, you get no extra money.

BAQ rates are set by rank. In fact, each rank has four different BAQ rates:

- One for people with family members who officially qualify as dependents
- A second for military members without dependents
- A third for servicemembers living in barracks or aboard ship or during field exercises, called the partial rate
- A fourth, called BAQ-Diff, for divorced military members whose only dependents are children living with the divorced spouse

The first three BAQ rates are part of the regular military pay chart. The fourth, BAQ-Diff, is calculated by a simple formula. To determine someone's BAQ-Diff rate, subtract that person's BAQ at the without-dependents rate from the BAQ at the with-dependents rate.

During 1997, BAQ at the with-dependents rate ranged from $361.50 a month for a new recruit to $1,015.20 for a four-star general or admiral. The without-dependents rate started at $202.50 a month for E-1s and topped out at $824.70 a month for O-10s.

The partial rate, usually received by people in barracks or aboard ship, started at $6.90 a month for a recruit and went up to $50.70 a month for a four-star officer in 1997.

BAQ rates are usually expressed as a monthly payment, but they can also be paid at a daily rate, which is one-thirtieth of the monthly rate per day. Reservists and guardsmen on active duty receive the daily rate whenever they don't serve a full calendar month on full-time status.

THE WITH-DEPENDENTS RATE

BAQ is one military payment that is tailored—in a limited way—to the size of a servicemember's family. If a relative lives with you under the same roof—or lives elsewhere, but you support that person financially—then you probably qualify for BAQ at the with-dependents rate.

Having just one other person in the household triggers eligibility for with-dependents BAQ. There's no additional money for two or more family members.

> If a family member has a military ID card, then you are probably entitled to BAQ at the with-dependents rate.

The family member can't be just anyone, however. That other person must meet the military's official definition of dependent. Usually, that includes spouses, parents who receive at least half their income from a military person, and children who are no older than twenty or who are disabled.

The children of divorced servicemembers who live with the civilian parent trigger eligibility for BAQ-Diff, discussed earlier.

THE PARTIAL RATE

Most military people without dependents are eligible for BAQ payment at the partial rate when they live in quarters provided by the government, such as in barracks, in dormitories, aboard ship, or in the field.

Reservists and guard members who don't have dependents and are on active duty for short stints, such as fourteen-day annual training, usually qualify for partial-rate BAQ, rather than BAQ at the without-dependents level. That's because the government provides them with housing.

TAXES

BAQ is tax free. This applies to state and federal income taxes, as well as taxes for Social Security and Medicare. This tax protection applies equally to the four different BAQ rates.

Taking advantage of this tax-free status doesn't require any effort on the part of military members. When the finance centers prepare annual summaries of every military person's tax records—officially known as the W-2 tax forms—they don't report any BAQ money as taxable income.

The tax-free nature of BAQ is unaffected by how it is used. You don't have to spend it on housing. If your housing costs are smaller than your BAQ payment, you can keep the difference, and it's still tax free.

DUAL-SERVICE COUPLES

When husband and wife are both on active duty, special care (and extra confusion) is involved in sorting out their BAQ. When husband and wife are in the reserves, that complexity can multiply.

As far as reservists and guardsmen are concerned, there are two important rules. First, when both spouses are officially on any category of active duty during the same calendar day, they face the same restrictions as any other dual-service active-duty couple drawing BAQ.

Second, if only one member of a two-member military family is on active duty and drawing BAQ for a calendar day, the military considers the non-active-duty spouse the same as any other spouse. This means that the military member on active duty should receive BAQ at the with-dependents rate.

The pay regulations discuss more than two dozen different kinds of circumstances affecting BAQ rates for dual-service couples on active duty.

SPECIAL CIRCUMSTANCES

A variety of factors—most of which involve one's active-duty status or official dependents—can affect whether someone is entitled to BAQ and whether it should be paid at the partial, without-dependents, or with-dependents rate.

Often, the only way to resolve a controversy is to ask. The pay regulations detail the rights of military members. Here's how those regulations treat some military personnel, especially reservists and guard members, in special circumstances:

Afield or Afloat: People on active duty with family members who qualify officially as dependents receive BAQ at the with-dependents rate, even when the military is providing the servicemembers with housing in the field or during sea duty.

Reservists and guardsmen without dependents can qualify for BAQ at the without-dependents rate, even though the government is housing them during exercises in the field.

Partial-rate BAQ goes to reserve-component members who are on active duty and meet the following three conditions:

- On sea duty
- E-6 or lower rank
- Without official dependents

Higher-ranking people without families who are on sea duty qualify for BAQ at the without-dependents rate.

AWOL: Servicemembers on active duty who are absent from their duties without permission lose BAQ payments for each day of the absence. This includes reserve-component members on active duty for a few days.

Boyfriends and Girlfriends: To qualify for BAQ at the with-dependents rate, a military member must have at least one other person in the household who officially qualifies as a dependent. Live-in boyfriends and girlfriends, even those who are totally dependent financially on the military member, aren't dependents.

> For a servicemember to qualify for BAQ at the with-dependents rate, the family member must meet the military's definition of "dependent."

Divorce and Children: Military members need only one official dependent to qualify for BAQ at the with dependents rate. Sometimes, that dependent is a child who lives with an ex-spouse.

To qualify for BAQ at the with-dependents rate, the servicemember must financially support the child. At a minimum, that support must equal the difference between the person's BAQ at the with-dependents rate and his BAQ at the without-dependents rate.

Divorce and Separation: A spouse from whom someone is legally or even informally separated can still be a dependent, as long as that spouse is financially supported by the military member. How much support is enough? Usually, the spouse must receive at least as much money as the member's BAQ payment.

Once a divorce is official, the spouse is no longer an official military dependent. The payment of alimony to an ex-spouse does not entitle a servicemember to BAQ at the with-dependents rate, nor does the payment of money for a community-property settlement.

Garnishment: BAQ is protected from collection by people to whom military folks owe money, specifically, any debts to businesses, as well as child support and alimony.

Hospitalization: Usually, active-duty members continue drawing BAQ if they're hospitalized. This also applies to reserve-component members hospitalized while on active duty.

Reservists and guard members hospitalized while on inactive-duty status for inactive-duty-related medical problems can receive BAQ as part of Incapacitation Pay.

Non-Support of Family: A commander can cancel a servicemember's with-dependents BAQ and insist on proof of support if a complaint is made that an active-duty member isn't financially supporting his dependents. That complaint can come from a dependent, a spouse, a chaplain, a child welfare agency, a relative, or a stranger.

4

BASIC ALLOWANCE FOR SUBSISTENCE

In This Chapter:

- *Eligibility*
- *Overview on Rates*
- *Rules for "On Leave"*
- *Rules for "Rations in Kind"*
- *Rules for "Emergency Conditions"*
- *Rules for Supplemental*
- *Rules for Prorated*
- *Taxes*
- *Special Circumstances*

When reserve-component members find themselves officially on active duty, they're eligible for Basic Pay. The rules are fuzzier for reservists and National Guard members qualifying for Basic Allowance for Subsistence (BAS). They can receive it for short stints on active duty, but it's not guaranteed.

BAS pays for the military member's food, but not the family's. It doesn't increase when a military member gains a family. Some rules seem unfair because they may result in the family having a smaller total take-home pay when the government feeds the military member.

ELIGIBILITY

BAS can be paid to any member of the reserve components who is officially listed as being on active duty. The length of time on active duty doesn't affect eligibility, nor does the length of time that the parent service originally intended to keep the reservist or guardsman on active duty.

BAS stops when the government feeds enlisted troops. Officers get BAS if the government feeds them, but they must pay for those government-provided meals, which wipes out the BAS.

Enlisted reservists on active duty for short stints, including the annual two-week period of active duty for training, are usually provided with meals. Thus, they don't receive BAS. However, even these reservists may be eligible for BAS payments while traveling to and from their active-duty sites.

Ineligible for BAS are reservists and guard members who are technically classified as being on inactive-duty status, which includes recipients of Drill Pay and members of the reserve components who are earning points for retirement by unpaid duties and training.

OVERVIEW ON RATES

BAS rates are unaffected by the actual costs of food. If you spend less for meals than you receive in BAS, you can keep the difference. However, if your food costs exceed your BAS payment, you get no extra money.

The BAS system is fundamentally different for officers and for enlisted members. Officers have only one BAS rate. Enlisted BAS is divided into three major categories, plus two additional categories that are less common.

BAS rates usually change every year, generally by the same percentage as Basic Pay.

Enlisted members can find themselves changing BAS categories during a single month on active duty, depending on where they're serving and the availability of government dining halls.

Officers: All commissioned officers and warrant officers receive the same amount of BAS. Rank, years of service, level of responsibility, and place of duty don't affect the amount. For 1997, BAS for officers was $154.16 a month.

When an officer is fed by the government, as is often the case with reservists and guardsmen during their two-week stints of active duty for training, the officer has to pay the government for his meals. Such meals include dining in a ship's galley, eating MREs (meals ready to eat) in the field, being served food in a military hospital, or eating in a unit's mess hall.

Officers in the field for training or for actual contingencies can receive per diem in addition to BAS.

Enlisted: Enlisted rates are broken down into three major categories and two minor ones. Each of those five categories, in turn, is divided into two segments—one for active-duty enlisted members with less than four months in uniform, and one for everyone else in the enlisted ranks.

BAS Summary

Purpose:	To pay for food away from government facilities
Amounts:	For officers, $154.16 a month (1997); for enlisted, from $6.79 to $10.99 a day (1997)
Rates:	One rate for officers, ten for enlisted
Taxable:	No
Loopholes:	Can draw both BAS and per diem
Problem areas:	When government provides food; on leave; drawing per diem

Enlisted BAS is strictly an active-duty benefit. Reservists and guard members training in inactive-duty status with their reserve-component units aren't eligible for BAS.

The three major BAS categories for enlisted people have cumbersome titles. They are:

- On leave or granted permission to mess separately (known informally as "sep-rats")
- Rations in kind not available
- Emergency conditions where no government messing is available

The two minor categories involve situations in which enlisted people eat some meals in a government dining facility and some in their homes, in restaurants, or at fast-food stores:

- Supplemental subsistence allowance
- Prorated subsistence allowance

Each service has its own rules for determining which category of BAS applies in which cases.

RULES FOR "ON LEAVE OR GRANTED PERMISSION TO MESS SEPARATELY"

Enlisted reservists traveling to and from an active-duty training site are often eligible for this kind of BAS. Eligibility isn't affected by whether the reservist actually receives BAS at the active-duty location.

In 1997, enlisted personnel receiving BAS under this provision got $6.79 daily if they had less than four months in the military and $7.36 daily if they had more time.

Among full-time active-duty people, this category of BAS is paid to those who are married, those living off base, and those living on base with enough rank so that they don't have to eat in military dining halls.

People in all these situations have been given, as the name states, permission to mess separately by their commanders or by the regulations of their service. This kind of BAS is nicknamed "separate rations," or "sep-rats."

As with other BAS recipients, those receiving separate-rations BAS normally aren't fed by the military. An exception was created in 1994. Enlisted members on what's officially classified as field duty are allowed to keep separate-rations BAS. Many reservists and guardsmen on active duty for a couple of weeks of training qualify for BAS under this provision.

The official definition of field duty has two parts. To qualify, enlisted members must be: (1) fed in a government mess or with field rations and (2) serving with troops on maneuvers, war games, field exercises, or similar operations.

RULES FOR "RATIONS IN KIND NOT AVAILABLE"

When there's simply no government dining facility where enlisted members on active duty can be fed, this is the category of BAS they receive.

In 1997, it amounted to $7.65 daily for people with less than four months on active duty and $8.30 daily for those with more time in service.

This category of BAS goes mainly to enlisted people who work off base, including reservists and National Guard members during short periods of active duty. If a government dining facility is available for some meals, then BAS under this category is reduced to take into consideration the meals that the military provides.

> In simple English, "subsistence in kind" and "rations in kind" mean "government-supplied food."

Often, a government dining facility is officially unavailable if it's more than thirty minutes away from the place a military person works. This is just a rough guideline.

BAS under this category doesn't go to servicemembers who are traveling to an active-duty assignment, even though they might not be able to eat in a government dining hall. Those cases are covered under "Rules for 'On Leave or Granted Permission to Mess Separately.'"

RULES FOR "EMERGENCY CONDITIONS WHERE NO GOVERNMENT MESSING IS AVAILABLE"

Occasionally, enlisted people find themselves in places where government-provided food isn't available and the usual BAS rate doesn't come close to paying for food.

For these situations, the government has established a special category of enlisted BAS. It's known informally as the Emergency Rations Rate, or ERR.

For 1997, the rates allowed $10.16 daily for an enlisted person with less than four months' service and $10.99 daily for everyone else.

Reservists and guardsmen on short periods of active duty rarely are eligible for BAS at the ERR level. Only a narrow set of circumstances justify the payment:

- The enlisted member has a temporary assignment expected to last less than 180 days.
- The assignment is within one of the contiguous forty-eight states.
- Government dining facilities are unavailable.
- The servicemember's room doesn't have cooking facilities.
- Payment has been approved by an official designated by one of the service secretaries.

RULES FOR SUPPLEMENTAL SUBSISTENCE ALLOWANCE

Sometimes, enlisted members are consistently unable to use government dining facilities because there aren't any near their place of duty.

Enlisted members given separate-rations BAS can sometimes qualify for an additional allowance for each meal they pay for out of their own pockets.

Called the supplemental subsistence allowance, it has different rates for each meal of the day. The rates are small, amounting in 1997 to less than $1.00 per day.

RULES FOR PRORATED SUBSISTENCE ALLOWANCE

When an enlisted member receiving BAS eats in a government dining hall, that person cannot collect BAS for that meal. The prorated subsistence allowance is the amount of BAS that a servicemember gets after having the cost of government-provided meals deducted from the daily BAS rate.

The amount of that loss depends on the meal and the kind of BAS being drawn. The per-meal rates are calculated in such a way that people eating three meals a day in government mess halls get bills that total 100 percent of their BAS, regardless of the kind of BAS they've been receiving.

TAXES

BAS is tax free. This applies to state and federal income taxes, as well as taxes for Social Security and Medicare. This tax protection covers all BAS rates.

Taking advantage of this tax-free status doesn't require any effort on the part of military members. When the finance centers prepare annual summaries of every military person's tax records—officially known as the W-2 tax forms—they don't report any BAS money as taxable income.

The tax-free nature of BAS is unaffected by how it is used. You don't have to spend it on meals. If your food costs are less than your BAS payment, you can keep the difference, and it's still tax free.

SPECIAL CIRCUMSTANCES

BAS has more fine print in its rules than do many types of military pay that involve more money. Here are some of the major implications that reservists and guardsmen need to know.

Advance Payments: Advance payment of BAS for members of the reserve components is rare. Normally, reservists and guard members don't qualify. However, reservists and National Guard members called to active duty for a national emergency may be paid up to three months' BAS in advance. The money must be repaid, or the finance center withholds all BAS earned in later months until the advance has been paid back.

Advance payments require the commander's approval. No one has a right to BAS advances, and commanders can limit the amounts to less than three months' worth.

AWOL: Military members lose their right to BAS payments if they're absent from their duties without proper authority. This applies to reservists and guardsmen, whatever their active-duty status.

Garnishment: BAS is protected from collection by people to whom military personnel owe money, specifically, any debts to businesses and child support and alimony payments.

Illness or Injury: Reservists and members of the National Guard who are injured or become ill while on active duty continue to receive BAS while hospitalized, although they may be charged for food served in a government hospital.

One of the first laws on military pay in 1790 set the pattern that money for rations wasn't included in pay.

If a disabling injury or illness occurs during an inactive-duty drill period, while traveling to a drill period, or while traveling home after a drill period, members of a reserve component may be authorized BAS as part of incapacitation pay.

Overseas COLA: The overseas cost-of-living allowance has no effect on BAS. BAS is not reduced because a servicemember collects an overseas COLA. Nor does the BAS rate affect the amount of COLA received.

Per Diem: Reservists and guardsmen who qualify for per diem can receive it in addition to BAS payments. Those who don't qualify for BAS—usually because they have been ordered to active duty without pay—cannot receive per diem.

Per diem payments are made to military personnel on temporary duty, on temporary additional duty, or traveling under orders to a new permanent assignment. Generally, enlisted people drawing per diem receive BAS at the separate-rations rate.

Without Pay: Reservists and National Guard members who are in the official category of being ordered to active duty *without* pay can receive BAS at the same rates as active-duty members while serving at their permanent-duty stations. While away from their permanent-duty stations, they receive only a token payment—$1.50 per meal in 1997—for food.

Members of a reserve component who come on active duty with orders that specifically say "without pay *and allowances*" are ineligible for any form of BAS.

5

CHANGES TO PAY

In This Chapter:

- *Advance Pay*
- *Allotments*
- *Garnishment*

A lot has changed since the days when military members were paid by officers who counted out the money in the field while using an up-ended drum as a table.

Most military pay now goes electronically from a finance center to a servicemember's bank. Mid-month pay periods, a rarity as recently as the Vietnam War, have become routine for most active-duty people. This chapter covers some of the other financial programs that have become important features of the military pay system.

ADVANCE PAY

It's not always possible to pay one month's bills with one month's income. This is especially true for reservists and guardsmen who must combine the financial burdens of moving with the extraordinary demands of going from the private sector to the active-duty world.

All services have provisions written into the regulations

that permit the advance payment of a military paycheck. Advance pay isn't a right, however. Commanders can deny a request for advance pay if it appears likely to create more financial problems than it solves.

Eligibility: Advance pay is limited to people on active duty or to reservists or guard members who are in the process of coming on active duty.

Members of the reserve components must fall into one of four categories to qualify for advance pay:

- Already serving on extended active duty
- Already on active duty after emergency mobilization
- Ordered to active duty for at least 140 days
- Ordered to extended active duty

The second category, covering reservists and guard members who've been mobilized, applies only when they're not paid within fourteen days of reporting to active duty.

Note that the last two categories open up advance pay to people not yet on active duty.

> Advance payment of Drill Pay isn't authorized.

Advance payment of Drill Pay or other kinds of military pay for services while on inactive-duty status isn't authorized.

Types: Advances can be made for Basic Pay, the Basic Allowance for Subsistence (BAS), the Basic Allowance for Quarters (BAQ), the Variable Housing Allowance (VHA), and the Overseas Housing Allowance (OHA).

Advance payment of Basic Pay comes under one set of rules, BAS under another, and housing-related allowances under a third set of rules.

Basic Pay: Servicemembers eligible for advance pay can receive one month's Basic Pay by applying to the finance office controlling their paychecks.

With their commanders' approval, military people can

receive up to three months' Basic Pay. Many commanders require written documentation of anticipated expenses that justify the advance payments. Commanders can also approve less than three months' advance, they can control when the servicemember receives the advance, and they can even order that the payment be made in installments.

When advance payments of Basic Pay are made, the amounts aren't the ones that appear in pay charts. Subtracted from each month's advanced Basic Pay are:

- Montgomery GI Bill contributions
- Federal and state income taxes
- Social Security taxes
- Premiums for Servicemember's Group Life Insurance (SGLI)
- Premiums for dependent dental plan
- Garnishments
- Court-ordered support payments
- Repayment of debts to the U.S. government

Subsistence: For reservists and guard members who meet the general eligibility rules for advance pay discussed earlier, up to three months of BAS can be paid in advance.

This is the toughest kind of advance pay to receive and the one over which commanders exercise the most control.

Housing: Three different housing allowances—Basic Allowance for Quarters (BAQ), the Variable Housing Allowance (VHA), and the Overseas Housing Allowance (OHA)—are payable in advance.

For military people stationed stateside, up to three months' BAQ and VHA may be advanced for unusual housing-related expenses. For people stationed overseas, normally one year's BAQ and OHA may be advanced, although commanders have the authority to approve larger advance payments.

Military members must be able to document these expenses in writing when making requests.

No one is guaranteed any advance housing payments. Prohibited are advance payments of housing allowances for costs related to purchasing a home or buying real estate.

Repayment: All kinds of advance pay must be repaid. Normally, repayment of advance Basic Pay, BAQ, VHA, and OHA are made in twelve equal installments, beginning the month after the advance payment.

Recipients of advance BAS payments lose all future BAS until the money has been repaid.

Servicemembers have the option of requesting a faster repayment schedule. The military requires faster repayment if a person is scheduled for discharge or retirement before the end of the twelve-month repayment period.

Recipients of exit bonuses who are scheduled for discharge in less than twelve months after receiving an advance can ask the government to collect the money owed from the exit bonus.

Commanders have the authority to approve twenty-four-month repayment plans in extraordinary circumstances when a speedier repayment would cause the servicemember severe economic hardship.

Servicemembers deployed aboard ship for more than thirty days can have their complete paychecks withheld until the advance pay is repaid.

ALLOTMENTS

An allotment is an amount of money that active-duty personnel instruct the finance center to deduct from their regular paychecks and pay directly to someone else. Allotments are especially helpful in ensuring that financial commitments are honored when servicemembers are deployed, on sea duty, or in the field when bills become due.

Eligibility: Reservists and National Guard members must usually be on certain kinds of long-term active duty to begin allotments.

Inactive duty: Allotments from Drill Pay and other military income from inactive-duty status are limited to:

• Reserve-component members paying premiums for a government-backed income-protection program.

• National Guardsmen paying premiums for state-sponsored life insurance programs.

Active duty: To qualify for the full range of active-duty allotments, reservists and guardsmen must be:

• Serving voluntarily on active duty for at least 180 days.

• Serving involuntarily on active duty for at least 24 months.

Reservists and members of the National Guard who pass through one of these active-duty eligibility hoops can authorize allotments as soon as they come on active duty. They don't have to wait 180 days or 24 months to begin their allotments.

Authorized Allotments: Everyone on active duty, including reservists on extended active duty, are eligible to have allotments drawn from their regular paychecks.

Ineligible are reservists and National Guard members officially on inactive duty and drawing Drill Pay or those on active duty for short periods of training.

The general rule is that military members can have six different allotments drawn from each military paycheck. But that number is misleading, because some allotments aren't counted against that limit.

The following allotments fall into the general category of payments that count toward the six total allotments. Finance professionals refer to them as discretionary allotments:

• Payments to spouses, dependents, ex-spouses, other family members, or financial institutions on behalf of these people

• Life insurance premiums

• Deposits to banks, savings and loans, financial institutions, mutual fund companies, and investment firms

• Mortgages or rent

• Repayment of loans

Another category of allotments, referred to as nondiscretionary, aren't counted against the six that each military member is allowed:

- Delinquent federal, state, or local income taxes
- Savings bonds
- Repayment of loans from military relief societies
- Repayment of government debts
- Charitable contributions to the Combined Federal Campaign or military relief societies

The military's involvement with allotments ends after the check has been written (or, more commonly, the money has been transferred electronically).

Computing Allotments: Most elements of a military paycheck can be tapped to provide an allotment, but there are limitations. Servicemembers must withhold enough money from allotments to pay their taxes and other obligations.

Following are the elements of a military paycheck that can clearly be included in allotments:

- Basic Pay
- Basic Allowance for Quarters
- Basic Allowance for Subsistence
- Diving Pay
- Family Separation Allowance (type II, FSA-R only)
- Flight Pay
- Foreign Duty
- Hostile Fire Pay
- Imminent Danger Pay
- Medical bonuses
- Overseas Cost-of-Living Allowance
- Overseas Housing Allowance
- Proficiency Pay
- Sea Pay
- Sign-up bonus for overseas extension
- Special Duty Assignment Pay

- Submarine Pay
- Variable Housing Allowance

Allotments cannot equal a servicemember's full, pretax military income. Finance centers must withhold from an active-duty member's allotments enough to pay:

- Federal and state income taxes
- Social Security taxes
- Debts to the government
- Premiums for Servicemember's Group Life Insurance
- Deductions for the Montgomery GI Bill

Commanders also have the authority to limit allotments. Typically, this authority is used for active-duty people with chronic financial problems.

Special Circumstances: Here's how the rules for allotments affect military people and their family members in some common situations:

Death: Allotments stop at the death of the servicemember. When the recipient of an allotment dies, any uncashed allotment checks are invalid, even if received before the recipient's death.

Duration: Except in specific instances, once an allotment is started, it continues until the servicemember stops it, is discharged, or dies on active duty. Exceptions to this rule involve repaid delinquent taxes, repaid debts to the government, and contributions to service relief organizations and to the Red Cross.

Mental incompetence: Allotments can be made to the guardians of mentally incompetent people or to the institutions caring for them but not to those disabled people directly.

Minors: Allotments can be made to the guardians or custodians of children under sixteen years of age but not directly to the minors themselves.

Power of attorney: People with formal power of attorney, even spouses, are unable to start, change, or stop allotments.

GARNISHMENT

When military members don't repay their debts, people with claims can take their cases to the government. The military is obligated to honor any court order calling for the finance center to pay creditors directly from a military member's paycheck. This process is called garnishment.

Who May Be Garnisheed: Basically, everyone receiving a military paycheck from the U.S. government can have a paycheck garnisheed.

This includes reservists and guardsmen on extended active duty, on short stints of active duty for training, and on inactive-duty status drawing Drill Pay and, in certain circumstances, retired reservists.

Reservists who qualify for retired pay but who haven't begun receiving it because they haven't reached age sixty cannot be garnisheed for military pay they're not receiving.

Who May Garnishee: Traditionally, military pay has been subject to garnishment for child support and alimony payments, settlement of debts with the government, and payment of delinquent income tax.

Since 1995, private creditors—both individuals and firms—have been able to seek court orders that call for garnishment from military paychecks.

> The military is an arm of the federal government. Expect it to enforce all court orders.

State laws in North Carolina, Pennsylvania, South Carolina, and Texas outlaw garnishment of military paychecks.

An agreement with the German government has given German courts power to approve garnishment claims against U.S. military paychecks.

How Much: Two different formulas are used to set limits on garnishment. When garnishment is sought to settle a private or business debt, creditors are limited to a maximum of 25 percent of a military member's disposable income.

When the garnishment is sought for child support, alimony, delinquent income taxes, and debts to the U.S. government, the finance center can send:

- Up to 50 percent of the servicemember's disposable income if the servicemember has remarried or supports a dependent child.
- Up to 60 percent of the servicemember's disposable income if the servicemember hasn't remarried and hasn't acquired a dependent child.
- An additional penalty of 5 percent of the servicemember's disposable income if the active-duty person is at least twelve weeks behind in payments.

Calculating Limits: Again, two different systems are used for determining disposable income.

For private and business creditors, the calculation of disposable income *cannot* include:

- Exit bonuses
- Housing Allowances (BAQ, VHA, or OHA)
- Retired Pay
- BAS

With these exceptions, the formula for determining a private creditor's 25 percent follows the general rules explained below.

For child support, alimony, delinquent taxes, and debts to the government, the following pay categories are included for determining disposable income subject to garnishment:

- Aviator Retention Pay
- Basic Pay
- Chemical Munitions Pay
- Crewmembers' Flight Pay
- Dangerous Viruses Pay
- Demolition Pay

- Disability Severance Pay
- Diving Pay
- Drill Pay
- Engineering and Scientific Pay
- Enlistment bonuses
- Exit bonuses
- Experimental Stress Pay
- Flight Pay (ACIP)
- Flight Deck Pay
- Foreign Duty Pay
- Foreign Language Pay
- Hostile Fire Pay
- Imminent Danger Pay
- Inactive-duty Pay
- Medical bonuses
- Non-Crewmembers' Flight Pay
- Nuclear-qualified pay
- Nursing pay
- Parachute Pay
- Proficiency Pay
- Reenlistment bonuses
- Responsibility Pay
- Retired Pay
- Sea Pay
- Sign-up bonuses (enlistment and reenlistment)
- Special Duty Assignment Pay
- Toxic Fuels Pay

The following pay categories are *not* included in the calculation of disposable income for garnishment:

- Basic Allowance for Quarters
- Basic Allowance for Subsistence
- Clothing allowances
- Family Separation Allowance
- Overseas Cost-of-Living Allowance

- Overseas Housing Allowance
- Travel allowances
- Uniform allowances

Finally, before allocating any money for garnishment, the finance center makes some high-priority withholdings from each military paycheck, including:

- Debts to the U.S. government
- Federal income tax
- Servicemember's Group Life Insurance premiums
- Social Security tax
- State income tax
- Survivor Benefit Plan premiums

Servicemembers' Rights: Servicemembers whose military pay has been targeted for garnishment have the right to notification by the military before action is taken.

They can present evidence to the finance center, especially evidence that the debt has been paid. (Remember, a garnishment claim has been supported by a court order, and the courts usually weed out frivolous cases.)

Military lawyers can provide advice, although they cannot represent a servicemember in court.

6

TAXES

In This Chapter:

- *Three Rules on Taxability*
- *Taxable and Nontaxable*
- *Combat-Zone Exclusion*
- *Federal Taxes*
- *State Taxes*
- *Social Security and Medicare*
- *Military Retirees*
- *Collection*

Members of the U.S. military are also members of U.S. society. With citizenship comes the responsibility to help pay the bills of government. Or, to put it more bluntly, even if you're wearing a uniform, you still have to pay the tax man.

What follows is only a summary; it doesn't cover everything you may need to know about the taxability of your military pay. Tax laws, especially in the states, are always changing. Make sure that you're basing your financial future on the latest version of all the facts.

THREE RULES ON TAXABILITY

First, military pay is usually taxable. That rule applies to federal income taxes, state income taxes, active-duty pay, inactive-duty pay, and retired pay. But as with many rules, there are exceptions:

Taxes are never paid on some parts of a military paycheck. Under tightly drawn conditions, parts—or all—of a military paycheck may be free from taxes.

Unless you know differently, however, you can't go wrong if you start your financial planning with the idea that everything that makes up a military paycheck will be taxed.

Second, if the federal government doesn't tax a particular type of military pay, neither will the states. In fact, states are frequently more generous than the federal government, exempting from state income taxes some military money that's subject to federal income taxes.

Third, you don't need a financial planner to take advantage of the nontaxable kinds of military pay.

If you've been receiving a nontaxable kind of military pay, such as BAQ, that money is simply not included by the government in the annual summary of your wages (the W-2 Form, Wage and Tax Statement).

In contrast, moving expenses and certain costs stemming from temporary duty can and should be deducted from income taxes. Individual taxpayers have the responsibility to ensure that they're not paying more in taxes than their obligations.

TAXABLE AND NONTAXABLE

Special tax breaks for military members protect the income of military personnel in combat zones. For the moment, let's look at how a military paycheck is treated during peace.

Tax Law Summary

Taxable:	Basic Pay, Drill Pay, most retired pay
Nontaxable:	Allowances, reimbursements for travel and moving, some disability retirement pay
Loopholes:	Combat-zone exclusion, tax-free states

Taxable: Unless the combat-zone exclusion is in effect, the following kinds of military pay are always taxable:

- Aviation Career Incentive Pay
- Aviator Retention Bonus
- Basic Pay
- Career Sea Pay
- Chemical Munitions Pay
- Continuation Pay for Aviation Officers
- Dangerous Viruses Lab Duty Pay
- Diving Duty Pay
- Demolition Duty Pay
- Drill Pay
- Enlistment bonus
- Experimental Stress Duty Pay
- Flight Deck Duty Pay
- Foreign Duty Pay
- Foreign Language Proficiency Pay
- Hazardous Duty Pay
- Hostile Fire Pay
- Imminent Danger Pay
- Inactive-duty Pay
- Leave pay
- Leave time (cashed in)
- Parachute Pay
- Reenlistment bonus
- Retired pay (nondisability)
- Sea Duty Pay
- Separation Pay
- Special Duty Assignment Pay
- Special pay for Nurse Corps officers
- Special Separation Benefit
- Submarine Duty Pay
- Toxic Fuels Duty Pay

- Toxic Pesticides Duty Pay
- Voluntary Separation Incentive

Nontaxable: The following kinds of military pay are always nontaxable:

- Basic Allowance for Quarters
- Basic Allowance for Subsistence
- Clothing allowances
- Family Separation Allowance
- Move-in Housing Allowance
- Per diem
- Overseas Cost-of-Living Allowance
- Overseas Housing Allowance
- Travel allowances
- Travel reimbursements
- Uniform allowances
- Variable Housing Allowance

Also in the nontaxable category are some important benefits that have a cash value, such as military health care, meals in military dining facilities, commissaries, exchanges, government housing, and other on-base services.

There are also payments from military members that have tax consequences. This includes money that the military withholds from pay for a variety of reasons. These payments are subtracted from paychecks before the finance center figures out how much money is owed for taxes. In this grouping are payments for:

- Dependent Dental Plan
- Montgomery GI Bill
- Servicemembers' Group Life Insurance (SGLI)
- Survivor Benefit Plan

Fuzzy Tax Status: The tax status of some kinds of military pay is difficult to summarize. They may or may not be taxable, depending on a variety of factors. These include:

- DITY (do-it-yourself) moving payments
- Disability retired pay
- Disability Severance Pay

Drill Pay: Drill Pay is always taxable for federal income tax purposes, unless a reservist or guardsman qualifies for the tax protections of the combat-zone exclusion, discussed below.

Some states offer limited tax-free status to inactive-duty pays, such as Drill Pay for National Guard members, especially during state call-ups as opposed to federal call-ups. Those states include:

- Kentucky
- Missouri
- Nebraska
- Pennsylvania
- South Carolina
- Virginia

COMBAT-ZONE EXCLUSION

Traditionally, when military members are sent into combat, the government agrees to forgive some—or all—of their responsibilities as taxpayers.

Federal and state income taxes are eliminated—or limited—by this tax break for military personnel, but the news isn't all good. Social Security and Medicare taxes continue to be collected from military paychecks while servicemembers are assigned to a combat zone.

Qualifying for these tax breaks requires the servicemember's physical presence in the combat zone, as is discussed later.

Except for air crews, few reservists and National Guardsmen find themselves assigned to a combat zone for drill periods or even for short stints of annual training on active duty. Usually, members of the reserve components must come on active duty for extended periods in order to get the assignments that qualify them for tax protection.

This provision, known officially as the combat-zone exclusion, is a creature of federal law. It becomes effective when the president signs an executive order that clearly and specifically states that he is invoking his legal powers to protect military pay from income taxes for those people serving in specific geographic areas.

Without that executive order, there are no tax breaks for military personnel under fire. In recent years, peacekeeping operations in Lebanon and Somalia and the invasions of Grenada and Panama were considered combat for many legal purposes but not for the combat-zone exclusion.

Since the end of the Vietnam War, only the Persian Gulf War and peacekeeping operations in Bosnia have resulted in the creation of a combat-zone exclusion for military taxpayers.

Amounts: The amount of the tax break from the combat-zone exclusion is different for officers and for the rest of the force.

Enlisted members and warrant officers have their military paychecks protected from federal and state income taxes for each month they're in the official combat zone.

Income tax protection for officers is decided by the top Basic Pay rate for E-9s. In 1997, the top enlisted rate was $3,478.50 a month. Officers serving in a combat zone could have only $3,478.50 a month shielded from federal and state income taxes in 1997.

Eligibility for this tax break and the amounts of money protected from the Internal Revenue Service (IRS) both come in one-month segments. An officer who serves one day in a combat zone has the same $3,478.50 of Basic Pay shielded from taxes as an officer who spends an entire month there. The same rule applies for enlisted members.

The Combat Zone: Each executive order authorizing the combat-zone exclusion gives a precise definition of the geographic area affected.

That definition usually includes the airspace above the designated countries and adjacent bodies of waters. Crew members aboard military aircraft flying immediately above any portion of the combat zone also qualify for income tax protection.

Combat-zone tax breaks don't apply to U.S. civilians, nor to the income that military members earn outside the combat zone, such as dividends on investments and interest from savings accounts.

Service in the Zone: It's not unusual for reservists and guardsmen on flight crews to qualify for the combat-zone exclusion during weekend drill periods by serving aboard aircraft that fly into the combat zone.

But there's an important distinction: you have to be there because the military sent you.

Not qualifying for the combat-zone exclusion are reservists and National Guard members who travel into the region as civilians, without any military status. Also not qualifying are active-duty personnel stationed outside the zone who travel into the region on leave.

Fine Print: What's not taxable is military income *earned* while serving in a combat zone. Money earned in a zone but not actually received until after a servicemember has left the zone benefits from the tax breaks of the combat-zone exclusion.

This tax break applies only to military income. Money earned outside the combat zone—investment income, interest on savings accounts, mutual fund proceeds—is still fully taxable.

FEDERAL TAXES

Except for tax-exempt allowances and pay for service inside an officially designated combat zone, the money that military people receive in their paychecks is subject to federal income taxes. Included are reservists and guardsmen receiving Drill Pay and other allowances for inactive duty during drill periods.

Like every other taxpayer, military members must ensure that money is withheld from each paycheck to meet their tax obligations. Also like other taxpayers, military people can increase or decrease the amount of that withholding to take into effect their personal circumstances. Finance offices have the forms to adjust the amount of withholding.

When military members fail to pay their federal taxes, the IRS can use special administrative procedures that enable it to collect the delinquent taxes directly from the military finance center.

In extreme cases, the IRS can even collect portions of a military paycheck that are normally tax-exempt, such as housing allowances or travel reimbursements. It can also collect money that the servicemember has designated for other purposes, such as payments for government-sponsored life insurance or the Montgomery GI Bill.

STATE TAXES

Each state decides whether to have a state income tax and, if so, what kinds of income to tax. Some states don't tax military income, including Drill Pay. Others treat military paychecks the same as any other.

The federal government imposes some limitations on the states. If a certain kind of military pay is protected from federal taxes, then it can't be taxed by a state either. Only one state can tax the military income of each servicemember for the same period of time.

When it comes to individual income taxes, states generally fall into four broad categories:

No Tax: States that don't have any personal income tax are:

- Alaska
- Nevada
- South Dakota
- Texas
- Washington
- Wyoming

Limited Tax: States that don't tax wages (such as a military paycheck) but do tax such things as capital gains, interest payments, stock dividends, or the value of property such as stocks and bonds are:

- Florida
- New Hampshire
- Tennessee

No Military Tax: States that don't tax military paychecks are:

- Illinois
- Michigan
- Montana

Limited Military Tax: Certain states won't tax military paychecks if the servicemember is a legal resident whom the military has stationed outside the state (which is an indirect way of saying that legal residents assigned to their home state must pay state income taxes on military income). They are:

- Pennsylvania
- Vermont

Keep in mind that reserve-component members with regular jobs will have that civilian income treated just like the income of any other civilian wage earner in the state.

SOCIAL SECURITY AND MEDICARE

Military members pay taxes to both Social Security and Medicare, and they're eligible to receive benefits from both systems. Social Security and Medicare taxes are automatically withheld from each military paycheck, using standard government formulas.

Reservists and National Guard members receiving Drill Pay have both Social Security and Medicare taxes automatically withheld from those paychecks. The income from their full-time civilian jobs, normally subject to Social Security and Medicare taxes, doesn't affect military withholding for these two taxes, nor do military withholdings affect what's done by civilian payroll offices.

> If "allowance" is part of a payment's official name, that usually means that it is not taxable.

Military retirees are eligible to receive Social Security and Medicare benefits under the same rules applicable to civilian wage earners. Military retired pay is free from Social Security and Medicare taxes.

Here are some more details about the military and Social Security and Medicare taxes:

• The combat-zone exclusion doesn't apply to Social Security and Medicare taxes. They are automatically withheld from income earned in a combat zone, even though other federal taxes and state incomes taxes don't apply there.

• Military pay earned during periods of illness, hospitalization, and absence from duty for medical reasons is subject to Social Security and Medicare taxes.

• Contributions to the Montgomery GI Bill aren't subject to Social Security and Medicare taxes.

• Servicemembers who lose Basic Pay or Drill Pay because of a court-martial sentence, an AWOL period, or confinement in a civilian jail don't have to pay Social Security and Medicare taxes on the withheld military pay.

MILITARY RETIREES

Military retired pay is considered taxable income. Except for a few disabled military retirees, people collecting military retired pay must pay federal income taxes.

States can tax military retired pay, but they don't have to (discussed later).

Social Security and Medicare taxes aren't collected from any military retired pay. Military retirees can receive Social Security and Medicare benefits without having that affect their retired pay. By the same standard, their military retired pay doesn't affect their right to receive benefits from Social Security and Medicare.

The tax obligations of military retirees require them to have money withheld monthly from their retired pay to pay their taxes. Like all taxpayers, however, they have some latitude in adjusting that amount to reflect their individual financial circumstances.

Military retirees who live outside the United States are still subject to federal income tax and are required to have monthly withholdings of their taxes.

Disability: Although the general rule is that military retired pay is taxable, there are some narrowly drawn exceptions. Military retired pay is what people receive after serving —usually—twenty years in uniform. Military disability retired pay is what people with between six and twenty years can get if wounds, injuries, or illnesses incurred in uniform have made them incapable of doing their jobs.

Military disability retirements operate under different rules from those of the normal military retirement system. Some military disability retired pay is tax-exempt, including that of:

- Retirees with disabilities related to injuries or illnesses incurred in combat.
- Retirees entitled to receive military disability retired pay on September 24, 1975, or at an earlier date.

• Retirees who were on active duty or within a reserve component on September 24, 1975, or at an earlier date.

Deductions: Several specific deductions are made from military retired pay before the finance center computes a retiree's tax obligations. This has the effect of lowering the amount of income that is taxed. These include:

• Contributions to the Survivor Benefit Plan (SBP)

• Reductions of retired pay under the Dual Compensation Act, which affects retirees who take second jobs as federal civil servants

• Contributions to the old Retired Serviceman's Family Protection Plan, an early version of the SBP

• Waivers of retired pay to collect VA disability compensation

This last item requires an explanation. Military members who can prove that their health was harmed by their service don't always qualify for military disability retirement. Most injured veterans receive VA Disability Compensation. It provides monthly payments from the Department of Veterans Affairs.

VA Disability Compensation is always exempt from all taxes. Military retirees can receive both VA Disability Compensation and retired pay at the same time, but for every VA dollar they receive, they must give up one military dollar.

State Taxes: As with the active-duty population, military retirees soon discover that the states fall into several major categories in their treatment of military retired pay.

States that don't have any personal income tax:

- Alaska
- Nevada
- South Dakota
- Texas
- Washington
- Wyoming

States that don't tax any military retired pay:

- Alabama
- Florida
- Hawaii
- Kansas
- Kentucky
- Louisiana
- Michigan
- Nevada
- New York
- Pennsylvania
- Tennessee

States that give a tax break to military retirees:

- Arkansas
- Colorado
- Delaware
- District of Columbia
- Illinois
- Indiana
- Maryland
- Mississippi
- North Carolina
- Ohio
- Oklahoma
- Oregon
- South Carolina

States that aren't listed above treat military retired pay the same as any other source of income, as least when it comes to collecting state income taxes.

A final warning for would-be tax wizards: Some intrepid retirees have tried to apply the combat-zone exclusion to retired pay. Their thinking works something like this:

If someone spent two years during a twenty-year career in a duly designated combat zone, that's 10 percent of a military career. They argue that 10 percent of that person's retired pay should be shielded from all taxes, because it was earned in a combat zone, where military pay is protected from all taxes.

It's an interesting argument, and it's tested periodically, but it's always unsuccessful. Legal experts say that the combat-zone exclusion clearly applies only to monthly paychecks received while in uniform.

COLLECTION

The government can—and will—order military finance centers to send portions of a delinquent taxpayer's military paycheck straight to an IRS office. That shift of your money is a straightforward administration process.

> Don't make important decisions with yesterday's legal advice. Laws change. Be sure to get the latest legal information.

It all begins if someone eligible for military pay, including Drill Pay, receives a formal IRS notice to pay overdue federal taxes. That starts a clock. If that person hasn't satisfied the tax collector within thirty days after receiving the notice, the government will order the finance center to start collecting the money from a person's military paycheck.

Once that automatic collection process begins the only way to avoid collection is to be:

- Serving in a combat zone that meets the definition of the combat-zone exclusion.
- Serving immediately outside an official combat zone that meets the terms of the combat-zone exclusion, and drawing Imminent Danger Pay or Hostile Fire Pay.
- Hospitalized because of injury, illness, or wounds incurred in an area meeting the combat-zone exclusion definition.
- Listed as missing.

For someone falling into one of these four categories, the collection process for delinquent federal taxes is put on hold. It begins again 180 days after the servicemember leaves the combat zone, leaves the hospital, or returns from being missing.

Servicemembers who retire owing a debt to the IRS can continue to make regular monthly payments from their retired pay. Others who simply leave the military are liable to see their last paychecks withheld by the government to satisfy the tax collector.

PART II

SPECIAL KINDS OF PAY

7

ENLISTED SIGN-UP BONUSES

In This Chapter:

- *Enlistment Bonus*
- *"Critical Specialties" Forgiveness*
- *Prior-Service Enlistment*
- *IRR and ING Enlistment*
- *Prior-Service Affiliation Bonus*
- *Reenlistment Bonus*
- *IRR and ING Reenlistment Bonus*
- *Designated Unit Pay*
- *Active-Duty Sign-up Bonus*
- *Active-Duty Reenlistment Bonus*

If the military wants you, sometimes it will pay to get you—even in the reserve components. All the services have special bonuses to entice people to join the reserves or the National Guard or to give those already in uniform a financial reason to stay around a few years longer.

These sign-up bonuses are unique to enlisted members. Officers with highly technical skills—usually pilots and medical officers—have incentives of their own, which are covered in the appropriate chapters of *Reservist's Money Guide*. The effects of reserve-component sign-up bonuses on active-duty enlistment and reenlistment bonuses are also discussed here.

ENLISTMENT BONUS

The armed forces have always offered financial incentives for people to join—or stay in—the reserves and the National Guard. The most widely used program is the enlistment bonus, technically known as Enlistment Bonus for the Selective Reserve.

Eligibility: Recipients of enlistment bonuses agree to join a drilling unit of the reserves or National Guard, or they make a commitment to join the trained manpower pool known as the Individual Mobilization Augmentation (IMA) program.

Enlistment bonuses go solely to those in the enlisted ranks who meet at least three broad criteria:

- Willing to serve at least six years
- High school graduate
- No previous military service

Not everyone who meets these three criteria receives an enlistment bonus. Each service has the authority to fine-tune the eligibility rules to meet its own needs.

Rates: The maximum is $5,000. The actual amount varies by service and by specialty.

Typically, the bonus is paid in installments. About half goes to new recruits at the end of their initial training in military skills, technically known as initial active duty for training (IADT). Each service has its own rules and procedures for paying the rest.

Repayment: Enlistment bonuses must be repaid if a servicemember doesn't serve the agreed length of time. The amount of the repayment is based on a straightforward principle.

For example, someone who has served four years of a six-year commitment has served two-thirds of the agreed time. That reservist or guard member must repay the government one-third of the enlistment bonus.

"CRITICAL SPECIALTIES" FORGIVENESS

Enlisted members who enter the reserves or National Guard with certain federally backed student loans may be eligible to have the military pay off those debts.

Eligibility: There are three major eligibility requirements:

• The reservist or National Guard member must possess a skill that the parent service officially recognizes as a "critical specialty."

• The reserve-component member must agree to serve with a drilling reserve unit or as a member of the manpower pool known as the Individual Mobilization Augmentation (IMA) program.

• The loan must be one of a handful of federally funded or federally insured student loans, including:

Auxiliary loans to assist students
Consolidated Loan program
Federal Insured Student Loans
Perkins Loans
SMART Loans
Stafford Loans
Supplemental loans for students

Among the people *not* eligible for this program are reservists and National Guard members who were already serving with a reserve-component unit or in the IMA program when they took out a federally backed loan.

Rates: Up to $10,000 in federally backed loans will be forgiven for qualified enlisted members (1997 rate).

The government has two ways of computing the rate of forgiveness. For each year of reserve-component participation, the government will forgive either 15 percent of the outstanding loan or $500, whichever is higher.

Interest continues to accumulate until a loan is completely paid off. Reservists don't have to repay the government for any part of the forgiven debt if they leave drill status or end their IMA participation.

Reservists or guard members participating in this loan-forgiveness program lose eligibility if they come on active duty. They receive fractional credit for their last year in the reserve components. That is, if they go on active duty at the end of March, when the calendar year is one-fourth over, they'll be credited with forgiveness for one-fourth the usual loan amount for that year.

PRIOR-SERVICE ENLISTMENT

People who've already served on active duty have skills and experience that the military wants in the reserves and the National Guard. A sign-up payment for these people is known as the Prior Service Enlistment Bonus.

Eligibility: This sign-up bonus is available to some—not all—reservists and guardsmen who meet the eligibility rules. The services have discretion in picking recipients. Recipients must:

- Agree to join a drilling reserve unit or the trained manpower pool known as the Individual Mobilization Augmentation (IMA) program.
- Commit themselves to three or six years in those reserve-component programs.
- Have less than ten years total military time.
- Possess an honorable discharge.
- Possess a military skill for which the bonus is offered.
- Not have previously received any reserve-related enlistment bonus, reenlistment payment, or extension-of-service pay.

Some fine print in the eligibility rules is important to reservists and guardsmen: ineligible are people who left active duty with an obligation to join the reserves or National Guard.

Rates: This bonus comes in two sizes: $2,500 for a three-year commitment, and $5,000 for a six-year commitment.

Generally, recipients receive half the money at sign-up time and the other half in evenly divided portions on the anniversary dates of their enlistment.

Repayment: Recipients of this bonus who don't serve the agreed-to length of time must repay the government for time not served. For example, someone who serves four years of a six-year commitment must repay one-third of the sign-up bonus.

IRR AND ING ENLISTMENT

Two important manpower pools are the Individual Ready Reserve (IRR) and the Inactive National Guard (ING). Both consist of trained, experienced personnel who aren't assigned either to a unit for regular drills or to a specific job that they would fill if mobilized. To keep them, the services offer a special bonus.

Eligibility: The individual services decide who gets the IRR or ING sign-up bonus and not everyone who is eligible receives it. Recipients must:

- Have no previous military service.
- Enlist for six years.
- Agree to go straight into the IRR or ING.
- Qualify in a combat or combat-support skill.

Rates: Eligible servicemembers receive a one-time sign-up bonus of $1,500.

Repayment: People who don't serve their obligated time must repay a portion of the bonus, based on time served. That is, someone who served only three years of a six-year commitment must repay half the bonus.

This repayment obligation affects those who leave the military, those who join a reserve-component unit, and those who come on active duty. In all three cases, the former IRR or ING member is not meeting the purpose of the bonus, which is to encourage people to serve in the IRR or ING.

PRIOR-SERVICE AFFILIATION BONUS

Not everyone who has an obligation to be in the reserves or National Guard has to serve with a unit. To encourage people to take their valuable skills into units where the military can put them to good use, the services offer the affiliation bonus.

Eligibility: The affiliation bonus is targeted at people who've already served on active duty—those with prior service. They must:

- Be eligible for reenlistment in the active-duty force.
- Agree to serve with a reserve unit or maintain a needed skill.
- Have a rank and skill for which the parent service has vacancies.
- Agree to serve with a reserve unit or in the trained manpower pool known as the Individual Mobilization Augmentation (IMA) program for the rest of their obligated time in uniform.

This bonus isn't available to full-time reservists or to members of the National Guard who are full-time technicians.

It's important to note that this sign-up bonus doesn't add any time to one's commitment to the reserve components. It just pushes those who are already there toward jobs where the military needs them.

Rates: The amount of an affiliation bonus is based on the amount of time a reservist or guard member is obligated to serve in the reserve components.

The rate is usually $50 for each month in the reserves or National Guard. Parent services have the authority to offer lower amounts.

Although the amount is calculated as a monthly rate, it's paid in one or two lump-sum payments. People obligated to spend less than eighteen months as a reserve-component member usually receive the full affiliation bonus when they sign a formal agreement. Those with obligations longer than eighteen months usually receive half when they sign the agreement and half on the fifth anniversary of their enlistment.

Repayment: People who don't serve their obligated time must repay a portion of the bonus, based on the amount of time served. That is, someone who served only one year of a three-year commitment must repay two-thirds of the affiliation bonus.

This repayment obligation affects those who leave the military, those who join a reserve-component unit, and those who come on active duty. In all three cases, the former reservist or guardsman is not meeting the purpose of the bonus.

REENLISTMENT BONUS

Some enlisted members who are already in the reserves may be eligible for a special sign-up bonus if they agree to stay a little longer. This extra money is called the Selected Reserve Reenlistment Bonus.

Eligibility: Recipients of this bonus must agree to serve with a drilling reserve unit or in a trained manpower pool as an Individual Mobilization Augmentation (IMA) program. Recipients must:

- Have less than ten years total military time.
- Possess a military skill—or agree to join a certain unit—for which the bonus is offered.
- Not have previously received any reserve-related enlistment bonus, reenlistment payment, or extension-of-service pay.

Enlisted members can receive this bonus only once during their military careers.

Rates: This bonus comes in two sizes: $1,250 for a three-year commitment, and $2,500 for a six-year commitment. Generally, half is paid at sign-up time, and the other half is paid in equal installments at anniversaries.

Repayment: Recipients who don't serve the agreed-to time must repay the government for time not served. For example, someone who serves four years of a six-year commitment must repay anything in excess of $1,650, which is two-thirds of the maximum $2,500 bonus.

IRR AND ING REENLISTMENT BONUS

Experienced reservists and guardsmen who aren't assigned either to a unit for regular drills or to a specific job that they'd be expected to fill if mobilized can sometimes qualify for a sign-up bonus.

Eligibility: Recipients must be members of the Individual Ready Reserve (IRR) or Inactive National Guard (ING) who agree to reenlist and spend more time in those manpower pools. They also must:

- Sign up for three or six years.
- Not have any remaining time-in-service obligations.
- Qualify in a combat or combat-support skill.

Reservists and guardsmen can receive this sign-up bonus only once.

Rates: Reserve-component members who agree to a six-year commitment can receive $1,500. Usually, there is an initial payment of $500, with the rest paid in equal annual installments.

A three-year commitment brings a maximum $750 bonus, paid in equal annual installments.

Repayment: Recipients who don't serve out their obligated time must repay a portion of the bonus, based on the amount of time served. That is, someone who serves only three years of a six-year commitment must repay half or $750.

DESIGNATED UNIT PAY

In order to attract people to units with a high likelihood of being mobilized during emergencies and to keep them once they've joined, the services offer a financial incentive called Designated Unit Pay or High Priority Unit Pay.

Eligibility: This sign-up bonus is available only to enlisted personnel in the reserves. Members of the National Guard are ineligible.

Recipients must be in a reserve unit that's been designated by the parent service for the extra pay. Payments are authorized for:

- Inactive-duty periods, or drill periods
- Unit training assemblies
- Equivalent training or instruction lasting at least four hours

Enlisted members of a designated unit may draw the pay for duties performed with another unit whose members aren't entitled to Designated Unit Pay. People in ineligible units can't receive the extra money even when they serve with one of the designated units.

Rates: The amount is set at $10 per drill period, regardless of rank, time in service, or job skill. Since the normal weekend drill consists of two official drill periods per day for two days, qualified reservists get an extra $40 in their paychecks for a weekend's service.

This money is subject to federal and state income taxes, but no Social Security tax is withheld.

ACTIVE-DUTY SIGN-UP BONUSES

There's a constant ebb and flow of people between the active-duty force and the reserve components. Under the right circumstances, reservists and National Guard members can qualify for active-duty enlistment bonuses, even if they've already spent time in uniform during drill periods and summer training.

> Receiving an active-duty sign-up bonus may affect one's eligibility for a reserve-component sign-up bonus.

Eligibility: Reservists and National Guardsmen can qualify for an enlistment bonus by signing up for the minimum—usually four-year—stint on active duty, as long as they meet the same eligibility criteria as civilians coming directly onto active duty.

> Sign-up bonuses from the reserves and National Guard may have to be repaid if recipients go on active duty.

Ineligible are members of the reserve components who have previously received an active-duty enlistment or reenlistment bonus.

Like many military financial programs, an enlistment bonus isn't a right. The military decides which skills justify the extra sign-up money.

Rates: The maximum enlistment bonus is $12,000. The military can offer smaller amounts.

Payment is made in installments. By law, the first payment cannot be more than $7,000. The rest of the bonus is paid in installments at least every three months.

Repayment: People who receive enlistment bonuses may have to repay the government for some or all of their sign-up money if they don't complete the amount of full-time service called for in their enlistment contracts.

Among the people subject to repayment are those who leave active duty before the expiration of their commitments to rejoin the reserves or National Guard. Usually, these people can keep the money they've received but aren't entitled to any more bonus money.

ACTIVE-DUTY REENLISTMENT BONUS

Reservists and National Guard members on active duty can receive reenlistment bonuses for continuing their full-time military service, under the same rules affecting everyone else on active duty.

But the active-duty reenlistment bonus, called the Selective Reenlistment Bonus (SRB), was designed for the active-duty population. It isn't easy for members of the reserve components to use their part-time service to qualify for SRBs.

Eligibility: Three factors are key in determining who can receive SRB payments:

- Military skill
- Time in service
- Amount of extra time to be spent on active duty

Time in the reserves or National Guard isn't counted for meeting minimum time-in-service rules. Time classified as active duty for training isn't counted either.

Reservists and National Guard members can receive SRBs if they reenlist for active duty within three months after being released from active duty. The reenlistment bonus isn't paid to people coming on active duty for training within this three-month grace period, nor for those whose official status was active duty for training when they left full-time service.

Usually, military members must have at least twenty-one continuous months on active duty—in a skill for which the military is offering extra money—to receive SRB payments.

Rates: The maximum reenlistment bonus that servicemembers can receive for committing themselves to another stretch on active duty is $45,000.

Actual amounts vary greatly, with the largest bonus going to people with the hardest-to-find skills.

Repayment: People who receive reenlistment bonuses may have to repay the government for some or all of their sign-up money if they don't serve the length of time called for in their enlistment contracts.

Among the people subject to repayment are those who leave active duty before the expiration of their active-duty commitments to rejoin the reserves or National Guard. Usually, these people can keep the money they've received, but aren't entitled to any more bonus money.

8

HAZARDOUS DUTY PAY

In This Chapter:

- *Hostile Fire or Imminent Danger Pay*
- *Hazardous Duty Pay Basics*
- *Chemical Munitions Pay*
- *Dangerous Organisms Pay*
- *Demolition Duty Pay*
- *Diving Pay*
- *Experimental Stress Pay*
- *Parachute Pay*
- *Toxic Fuels Pay*
- *Toxic Pesticides Pay*

Military life is surrounded by risks that don't diminish because someone is only a part-time member of the armed forces. Reservists and National Guard members are often subject to the same dangers as full-time military personnel, and they are eligible for many of the same payments related to hazardous duty.

Reserve-component members are treated the same way as any other full-time servicemember while on active duty, but people on weekend drill periods, active duty for training, and other short periods of active duty may find themselves limited by the fine print in the rules.

HOSTILE FIRE OR IMMINENT DANGER PAY

It used to be called combat pay—that extra money paid to military personnel who were under fire. The name has changed—now it is called either Hostile Fire Pay or Imminent Danger Pay—but the purpose is the same.

Hostile Fire Pay Summary

Purpose:	Financial recognition for extra risks
Amounts:	$150 a month (1997)
Rates:	Same for officers and enlisted
Taxable:	Generally, yes
Garnishment:	Yes
Loopholes:	Qualifying for one day results in full month's payment
Problem areas:	Combat-zone exclusion

Eligibility: Reserve-component members performing a wide variety of service—extended active duty, active duty for training, and even inactive-duty status during weekend drill periods—can qualify for Hostile Fire Pay.

As a practical matter, most recipients are on extended active duty.

Not eligible for Hostile Fire or Imminent Danger Pay are reserve-component members who meet one of the following definitions:

- Those not being paid for their service (those technically on nonpay status)
- Those who traveled into an area approved for this extra pay while on leave
- Those who traveled into an area approved for this extra pay as civilians

• Those who traveled through an approved area, in some military capacity, while going from one point outside the area to another point outside the area

This last category covers people who are passengers aboard military aircraft or ships that pass through a geographic region approved for Hostile Fire or Imminent Danger Pay but who don't take part in military operations inside the area.

Most servicemembers receiving Hostile Fire Pay get it because the Pentagon has established a specific geographic area in which everyone in uniform is eligible for the extra money.

There is also a second route to eligibility. It depends on a case-by-case determination by the military that U.S. servicemembers are in danger of coming under hostile fire.

This case-by-case eligibility for Hostile Fire Pay is usually determined not on an individual basis but in terms of naval vessels, aircraft, and ground units. If anyone on a vessel or aircraft becomes eligible for this extra pay, everyone does.

Rates: Hostile Fire Pay and Imminent Danger Pay comes in one size. In 1997, it was $150 a month. That amount goes to officers, warrant officers, and enlisted personnel, active-duty members, reservists, and National Guard members.

> Hostile Fire Pay and Imminent Danger Pay are two names for the same payment.

The amount of the payment doesn't change to keep up with inflation, military pay raises, or any other factor. In fact, the payment traditionally stays the same for many years.

With a few exceptions, everyone receiving this extra pay gets the full monthly rate as long as they qualify to receive it for at least one day in a calendar month.

Only one month's Hostile Fire Pay can be received in any calendar month. For example, if a servicemember left an area designated for the extra pay on June 15 and returned on June 28, that person would receive only the basic $150 monthly rate.

For those who qualify on the case-by-case basis, a full month's Hostile Fire Pay would be received for a single officially recognized instance of hostile fire. Getting shot at twice in one calendar month results in only one month's payment.

Taxes: Hostile Fire or Imminent Danger Pay is fully taxable. Like other portions of a military paycheck, it is protected from income taxes only when earned in a geographic area officially designated by the president as a tax-free zone for military pay.

When Hostile Fire Pay is authorized for serving within a specific geographic region, that region may or may not be a presidentially established tax-free zone. These geographic designations are two different things.

HAZARDOUS DUTY PAY BASICS

With the exception of Hostile Fire or Imminent Danger Pay, the other kinds of hazardous duty pay mentioned in this chapter share many of the same rules. In fact, they're officially lumped together as Hazardous Duty Incentive Pays, or HDIPs.

To save space and avoid repetition, first we'll look at the general rules that apply to all these HDIPs. Then, we'll consider some of the specific rules peculiar to each one.

Eligibility: Reserve-component members classified as being on extended active duty qualify for hazardous duty pay under the same rules as other members of the full-time military.

Reservists and National Guard members on some other kinds of active duty—such as active duty for training, annual training, and initial training tours for enlisted people without previous military service—can also receive hazardous duty pay if they meet the other eligibility criteria.

Members of the reserve components who are officially on inactive-duty status—which normally means that they're attending monthly drill periods or training authorized for members of the Individual Mobilization Augmentation (IMA) program—can receive only certain kinds of hazardous duty pay, including:

- Demolition Duty Pay
- Experimental Stress Duty Pay
- Flight Deck Duty Pay
- Parachute Duty Pay

Inactive-duty recipients of these pays must meet the same eligibility rules as active-duty personnel. For them, payments are usually calculated on a daily basis.

Reserve-component members officially on without-pay status are ineligible to receive any of the hazardous duty pays, even if they perform the dangerous tasks for which the extra money is authorized.

Rates: With one exception, the rate for the hazardous duty pay is $110 a month (1997 rate), for both officers and enlisted personnel in the active-duty force and the reserve components.

The only people who receive more are some parachutists who regularly jump at extremely high altitudes and open their chutes at extremely low altitudes. They can qualify for an extra $165 a month (1997 rate).

For periods of eligibility less than an entire month, which commonly apply to reserve-component members, the daily rate is $3.67.

Some military personnel may qualify for more than one kind of hazardous duty pay, but the regulations impose a limit. Military members, including reservists and guardsmen, can receive two of the hazardous duty pays mentioned below, plus Hostile Fire or Imminent Danger Pay.

The rates for these hazardous duty pays rarely change.

CHEMICAL MUNITIONS PAY

All weapons used by the military are dangerous. A few are commonly recognized as involving hazards that exceed the risks normally associated with military life. When these extra risks involve working around chemical weapons, military personnel are eligible for additions to their paychecks.

Eligibility: Recipients of Chemical Munitions Pay must be in military jobs whose primary tasks involve, according to the regulations, "the direct physical handling" of chemical munitions.

This handling can involve the storage, maintenance, testing, assembly, disassembly, disposal, or transportation of chemical weapons.

The most common kinds of contact with chemical weapons, and the most common chemical weapons, clearly fall short of meeting the eligibility test for this extra money. Kinds of service that *do not* qualify for this additional pay are:

- Working with riot-control gas, defoliants, smoke-producing materials, or flame-producing materials
- Loading shells or bombs containing chemical munitions into artillery tubes, aircraft, or other delivery systems
- Being in contact with chemical weapons during storage in the field
- Handling individual components of so-called binary weapons
- Conducting laboratory tests on the materials used in chemical munitions

Reminder: Chemical Munitions Pay is part of a larger package of hazardous duty pays. For more details, check the "Hazardous Duty Pay Basics" section on page 81.

DANGEROUS ORGANISMS PAY

Some of the most frightful weapons in the inventories of military forces are normally stored in laboratory test tubes. For military people who work every day with deadly viruses and bacteria, the Pentagon maintains a special category of hazardous duty pay. Some know it as Dangerous Viruses Lab

Pay or Dangerous Bacteria Lab Duty Pay, but the most common name is Dangerous Organisms Pay.

Eligibility: Dangerous Organisms Pay goes to military members assigned for at least thirty consecutive days to a laboratory in which their primary duty involves working with organisms for which no form of immunization is available.

Reservists and National Guard members on active duty can qualify for Dangerous Organisms Pay as long as they meet this thirty-day requirement and other provisions. The thirty-day rule makes ineligible reserve-component members drawing Drill Pay on inactive-duty status.

Dangerous Organisms Pay goes to people with direct, immediate, constant exposure from handling these deadly materials. Merely working in the vicinity of these viruses and bacteria does not qualify someone for this hazardous duty pay.

Reminder: Dangerous Organisms Pay is part of a larger package of hazardous duty pays. For more details, check the "Hazardous Duty Pay Basics" section on page 81.

DEMOLITION DUTY PAY

High explosives are a deadly part of military life. Demolition Duty Pay is a well-deserved addition to the military paychecks of the men and women who deal with some of the most powerful tools in the military's arsenal.

Eligibility: Military members eligible for Demolition Duty Pay have as their primary duty the use of high explosives.

The regulations mention four specific categories of military jobs that are eligible for Demolition Duty Pay, all sharing the requirement that military members work full time with explosives:

- Using explosives to demolish objects, obstacles, or other explosives
- Disarming explosives
- Serving as instructors in the use of demolitions, provided the instruction includes the use of live explosives

• Overseeing proficiency training for other demolitions workers, provided that live explosives are used

This is one of the hazardous duty pays that reservists and guardsmen can receive during monthly drill periods with their reserve units, as long as they meet the normal eligibility rules. They're paid on a daily basis.

Reminder: Demolition Duty Pay is part of a larger package of hazardous duty pay. For more details, check the "Hazardous Duty Pay Basics" section on page 81.

DIVING PAY

One of the most dangerous places on the planet is below the waves. For military people who work in that deadly environment, Diving Pay recognizes the risks incurred and the professional requirements involved when one works far beneath the ocean's surface.

Eligibility: Diving Duty Pay is directly linked to Basic Pay. Those not drawing Basic Pay can't get Diving Duty Pay.

Reserve-component members on full-time active duty or other kinds of active duty can receive Diving Duty Pay, as long as they meet the other eligibility requirements.

Ineligible are reservists and National Guard members who are drawing Drill Pay, serving on inactive-duty status, or serving in without-pay status on active or inactive duty.

Each service has regulations governing Diving Pay that are tailored to meet the needs of the service. Generally, there are separate rules and rates for officers and enlisted members.

Rates: Each service has a fairly complicated system that sets different rates for divers, based on the diving jobs they perform, skill level, and kinds of units to which they're assigned.

The minimum Diving Pay for all military members is $110 a month. The top enlisted rate is $300 a month, with only a handful of each service's best-qualified divers receiving the maximum. Officers are limited to a maximum payment of $200 a month, although only a few diving-qualified officers receive the maximum.

Split Hairs: Technically, Diving Pay isn't classified by the military as a hazardous duty pay. It was placed in this section because that's where most people expect to find it.

Recipients of Diving Pay can receive Hostile Fire or Imminent Danger Pay plus only one of the other hazardous duty pays mentioned in this chapter.

EXPERIMENTAL STRESS PAY

A handful of military assignments require military personnel to subject themselves to harsh physical conditions as part of medical experiments or to work in special pressure chambers helping deep-sea divers. For them, the Defense Department offers Experimental Stress Pay.

Eligibility: Reserve-component members who meet the normal eligibility rules can qualify for Experimental Stress Pay while on active duty.

Also eligible are reservists and National Guard members on inactive-duty status, which normally includes reserve drill periods or equivalent training for members of the Individual Mobilization Augmentation (IMA) program.

Recipients must meet narrowly targeted criteria. Eligibility for this kind of hazardous duty pay is limited to military personnel with three specific kinds of duty:

- Those who are the research subjects in acceleration or deceleration experiments
- Those who are the research subjects in so-called thermal experiments involving extremes of heat or cold
- Those who serve inside high-pressure or low-pressure chambers as research subjects, technicians servicing equipment, or instructors

This last category applies to many Navy people who use high-pressure chambers to train and to give medical care to deep-sea divers. The Navy's rules have further restrictions and requirements for so-called instructor-observers.

Reminder: Experimental Stress Pay is part of a larger package of hazardous duty pays. For more details, check the "Hazardous Duty Pay Basics" section on page 81.

PARACHUTE PAY

Parachute Pay comes in two categories: a regular rate based on usual military parachute jumps with static cords, and a higher rate for those who bail out at high altitudes with parachute openings at lower altitudes, called HALO jumps.

Eligibility: Reserve-component members on full-time active duty, active duty for training, and other kinds of active duty can qualify for Parachute Pay under the same rules as everyone else on full-time military service.

Reservists and National Guard members on inactive-duty status, which normally includes reserve drill periods or equivalent training for members of the Individual Mobilization Augmentation (IMA) program, can also receive Parachute Pay.

A key eligibility rule for Parachute Pay is that the servicemember must be assigned to a position that requires parachute jumps. Being a member of a civilian parachute club doesn't qualify a reservist or guard member for this extra money.

Reservists and guardsmen who are on jump status in their reserve-component units don't qualify for Parachute Pay while on active duty unless parachuting is required by their active-duty assignments.

Generally, servicemembers must bail out of aircraft once every three months to be entitled to Parachute Pay.

Recipients of the HALO rate must have undergone training in free-fall operations through a course that's either run by the military or officially recognized by the military. They must also meet the one-jump-in-three-months rule.

Rates: The normal monthly rate for Parachute Pay is $110. For those qualifying for the HALO rate, it's $165.

Reservists and guardsmen who qualify while on inactive-duty status receive the same rate as active-duty personnel.

Parachutists who qualify for both rates in a calendar month receive the higher HALO rate. No one receives two payments of Parachute Pay for the same month. The monthly rate is converted to a daily rate for those starting or leaving parachute status.

Reminder: Parachute Pay is part of a larger package of hazardous duty pays. For more details, check the "Hazardous Duty Pay Basics" section on page 81.

TOXIC FUELS PAY

The men and women who handle highly toxic materials used to power aircraft or missiles have their own kind of hazardous duty pay. A word of caution: The definition of "toxic fuels" used in this program is very precise. It doesn't apply to the fuels used in most military vehicles, aircraft, or missiles.

> Many hazardous duty pays are given at one-thirtieth the monthly rate for each drill period.

Eligibility: Reservists and guardsmen on active duty who have as their primary duty the handling of some specific, unusually dangerous fuels are entitled to extra money in their military paychecks. These fuels include:

- H-70
- Inhibited red-fuming nitric acid
- JP-X
- Liquid oxidizer–nitrogen tetroxide
- Unsymmetrical dimethyl hydrazine

Military officials can identify other kinds of toxic fuels that qualify people for Toxic Fuels Pay.

Reserve-component members on inactive-duty status cannot qualify for this extra money, nor can others on active or inactive duty who are merely in the vicinity of these hazardous materials. This pay program was set up to compensate those who work with these dangerous materials, up close, every day.

Reminder: Toxic Fuels Pay is part of a larger package of hazardous duty pays. For more details, check the "Hazardous Duty Pay Basics" section on page 81.

TOXIC PESTICIDES PAY

Uniformed personnel who work with the poisons used to control insects and other pests have their own kind of hazardous duty pay. Called Toxic Pesticides Pay, it is usually given to people who handle some specific deadly chemicals involved in fumigation.

Eligibility: Reserve-component members on active duty can qualify for this extra pay, as long as they meet the eligibility rules that apply to the rest of the force.

Reservists and National Guard members on inactive duty are ineligible, regardless of their exposure to these chemicals.

Recipients of Toxic Pesticides Pay are commonly assigned to military units involved with entomology, pest control, pest management, or preventive medicine. They must have regular exposure to certain highly toxic pesticides used in fumigation.

Solid chemicals used outdoors against burrowing animals are specifically cited in the regulations as *not* making military personnel eligible for Toxic Pesticides Pay.

Reminder: Toxic Pesticides Pay is part of a larger package of hazardous duty pay. For more details, check the "Hazardous Duty Pay Basics" section on page 81.

9

SPECIAL SKILLS PAYS

In This Chapter:

- *Special Duty Assignment Pay*
- *Foreign Language Pay*
- *Engineering and Scientific Pay*

Not all military jobs are equal. Some require skills that are difficult to acquire and tough to maintain. The services have a number of bonuses to attract and retain the right people for some hard-to-fill jobs.

This chapter considers the basic rules for some of these programs. Other kinds of payments can be found in Chapters 10–12.

SPECIAL DUTY ASSIGNMENT PAY

Some active-duty people have skills that their services have decided are worth extra money. The additional income is called Special Duty Assignment Pay, which some people still call Proficiency Pay or Pro Pay, a similar program that ended in 1984.

Eligibility: Reservists and National Guard members on extended active duty can qualify for this extra money, as long as they meet the other eligibility rules.

Reserve-component members on other kinds of active duty must be committed to spend at least 180 days in full-time service to qualify.

Ineligible are reservists and National Guardsmen on inactive-duty status, such as participants in weekend drill periods or comparable training.

Recipients must have a rank of E-3 or a higher enlisted rank. Commissioned officers and warrant officers are ineligible.

Once a military skill has been identified as qualifying for this bonus, everyone with the same Military Occupational Specialty (MOS), Air Force Specialty Code (AFSC), rating, career field, or occupational field is entitled to extra money.

Rates: Payments for Special Duty Assignment Pay are made monthly, as part of the regular military paycheck.

There are five possible amounts, based on the military's judgment about the degree of difficulty. Here are the rates in effect for 1997:

- SD-1, $ 55
- SD-2, $ 110
- SD-3, $ 165
- SD-4, $ 220
- SD-5, $ 275

These rates tend to stay the same for many years.

FOREIGN LANGUAGE PAY

Since 1987, a program has been on the books to encourage military members to learn, retain, and improve their language skills. Officially called Foreign Language Proficiency Pay, it's commonly referred to simply as Foreign Language Pay.

Eligibility: Reservists and National Guard members on extended active duty and shorter periods of active duty can qualify for this extra money, as long as they meet the other eligibility rules.

Reservists and National Guard members on inactive-duty

status, which includes weekend drill periods and comparable training, can receive Foreign Language Pay for their part-time service.

All recipients must meet an unusually large number of eligibility requirements including:

- Their military skill requires language proficiency.
- The job they're assigned to requires language proficiency.
- They know a language for which the military has authorized the extra pay.
- They've undergone language training recognized by the Department of Defense.
- They meet and maintain proficiency standards set up by the military, including an annual certification.

Rates: The military assigns linguists to one of four skill levels, each with its own monthly rate. Here are the rates in effect for 1997:

- FLPP-1, $ 25
- FLPP-2, $ 50
- FLPP-3, $ 75
- FLPP-4, $ 100

These rates rarely change.

Reservists and guardsmen on all categories of active duty have the monthly rate converted to a daily rate for their first and last months of eligibility.

Reserve-component members on inactive-duty status receive the daily rate—that is, one-thirtieth of the monthly rate appropriate for their skill level—for each drill period they attend.

Inactive-duty reservists and National Guard members who are credited with four drill periods in a month using their language skills receive a bonus equal to another one-thirtieth of the monthly Language Pay rate. Thus, five-thirtieths of the monthly rate is paid to the military's part-time linguists who amass four drill periods in a month using their language skills.

ENGINEERING AND SCIENTIFIC PAY

When no other financial inducement is available to persuade highly trained military members to spend time in uniform, the services can offer Engineering and Scientific Career Continuation Pay to people who stay proficient in their skills and remain on active duty.

Eligibility: Only commissioned officers on active duty qualify for this financial bonus.

Reservists and National Guardsmen on extended active duty can qualify for Engineering and Scientific Pay under the same rules that apply to the rest of the armed forces.

Reserve-component members on shorter stretches of active duty—active duty for training or annual summer training camp—are ineligible, even if they possess a skill for which the military is offering the bonus.

Members of the reserve components on inactive-duty status, such as weekend drill periods or comparable training, are also ineligible.

The military identifies the skills for which it will pay the bonus. Each service administers this program differently.

Rates: The maximum payment under this program is $3,000 a year for each additional year in uniform. Smaller amounts can be offered.

Military officials also have latitude in deciding how it will be paid—either as a lump-sum yearly bonus, as quarterly payments, or as regular portions of the monthly paycheck.

Repayment: Recipients who leave active duty before the end of their formal commitments must repay the government a percentage of the bonus, based on the portion of their obligations that they've fulfilled. This requirement for repayment cannot be avoided by recipients who join the reserves or National Guard.

10

FLIGHT PAYS

In This Chapter:

- *ACIP or Flight Pay*
- *Mid-Career Aviator Bonus*
- *Crewmembers' Flight Pay*
- *Non-Crewmembers' Flight Pay*
- *AWACS Flight Pay*

The armed forces offer extra money to military people for three basic reasons: because they do things that are dangerous, because they have skills that are technically demanding, and because they have skills that are sought by the private sector. When it comes to flying, all three reasons come into play.

Several different kinds of flight pay are on the books that recognize the skills and risks involved in operating military aircraft. Reserve-component members may qualify for extra pay while on active duty, during weekend drill periods, or during some combination.

ACIP OR FLIGHT PAY

Since 1974, Flight Pay has technically been known as Aviation Career Incentive Pay, or ACIP. Generally, it's restricted to people whose jobs are in the cockpit of an aircraft. Other military people whose duties require them to be in airplanes or helicopters have their own versions of flight pay, which are discussed later in this chapter.

Eligibility: Only commissioned officers and warrant officers are eligible for ACIP Flight Pay. Enlisted members are ineligible.

Reserve-component officers who are on extended active duty qualify under the same rules as the rest of the full-time military. Those rules are complex.

Reservists and National Guard members on other kinds of active duty—such as active duty for training, annual training, or temporary active duty—can also receive ACIP Flight Pay if they meet the active-duty rules. Generally, they must accumulate four flight-hours per month.

Members of a reserve component who are on inactive-duty status, such as those serving in monthly drill periods or equivalent training, can also qualify for ACIP Flight Pay. They must fly at least two hours per month.

The same hour of flight can be counted only once for ACIP Flight Pay.

A flight-hour performed on inactive duty can be applied to meet the minimum flight hours of someone on active duty, but flight hours accumulated on active duty cannot be used to earn ACIP Flight Pay for a reservist or guardsman on inactive-duty status.

Generally, the only flight-hours recognized by the military are ones earned in military aircraft by personnel assigned to flight units and performing what the regulations call "operational flying requirements."

Rates: Initially, ACIP recipients receive flight pay based on their number of years of aviation service, a period that begins with the first day in flight school. This aviation-based ACIP formula, called "phase one" by the military, is as follows:

Years of Flying	*Monthly Rate*
2 or less	$125
Over 2	156
Over 3	188
Over 4	206
Over 6	650

ACIP Flight Pay for warrant officers is always based on this phase one formula. Most commissioned officers receive their ACIP under the maximum category—"over 6"—for most of their careers. Note that rank isn't a factor in determining the amount of ACIP Flight Pay.

When a commissioned officer reaches the eighteenth anniversary of entering the military, the ACIP formula changes. No longer is it based on years as a flier, but years spent as an officer.

The "phase two" ACIP formula is as follows:

Years as an Officer	*Monthly Rate*
Over 18	$585
Over 20	495
Over 22	385
Over 25	250

An officer with more than eighteen years' commissioned time but less than six years' aviation time is entitled to the more generous aviation-based ACIP of phase one.

ACIP rates aren't subject to annual change. In fact, they tend to remain static for many years.

MID-CAREER AVIATOR BONUS

The military has a financial program targeted at mid-career flight crews that's called the Aviator Retention Bonus. It's tough for any reserve-component member, except those on lengthy periods of extended active duty, to qualify.

Eligibility: The Aviator Retention Bonus has several layers of eligibility rules. The most crucial one for reservists and National Guard members is that the bonus is for people who commit to serve additional periods on active duty.

Ineligible are people who are strictly on inactive-duty status, such as those who drill every month with reserve and guard units or those assigned to the special manpower pool known as the Individual Mobilization Augmentation (IMA) program.

Recipients must have at least six years on active duty, but they cannot have completed their thirteenth year on active duty.

In 1997, the Army and Coast Guard didn't offer Aviator Retention Bonuses to anyone. The Air Force offered it to all flight crews.

The Navy offered it only to crews of certain aircraft who agreed to extend their military commitments to reach their fourteenth year of service. The Marine Corps gave the Aviator Retention Bonus only to people increasing their commitments by one or two years.

Rates: The Aviator Retention Bonus comes in two sizes:

Short-term bonus: A maximum of $6,000 annually for officers who agree to extend their military obligations by one or two years.

Long-term bonus: A maximum of $12,000 annually for officers who extend their military commitments however long it takes to reach fourteen years of service.

If an officer is eligible for both, the aviator gets the more generous long-term bonus. Any officer who receives a bonus and fails to serve the full term of the commitment must repay the government for the unserved remainder.

CREWMEMBERS' FLIGHT PAY

Not everyone assigned to a military aircraft works in the cockpit. Other enlisted members of an aircraft crew are entitled to a special bonus that's usually called Crewmembers' Flight Pay; the formal name is Hazardous Duty Incentive Pay for Flying Duty.

Eligibility: Enlisted members of the reserve components are eligible to receive this extra money while on extended active duty, during other forms of active duty, and while on inactive-duty status.

Recipients must be under orders that call for "regular and frequent aerial flights as crew," according to the regulations. Usually, it goes to enlisted members serving aboard cargo aircraft.

One flight qualifies reservists for the full monthly rate for some flight pays. For others, the monthly rate is broken down into a daily rate. Some require minimum flight-hours during fixed periods.

A larger, separate bonus applies to enlisted members serving aboard Airborne Warning and Control Systems (AWACS) aircraft. The AWACS Flight Pay is discussed below. No one can receive both Crewmembers' Flight Pay and AWACS Flight Pay for the same flight.

Reservists and National Guard members on active duty must accumulate four flight-hours a month to qualify. People on inactive-duty status need only two flight-hours a month.

Reserve-component members must meet other eligibility rules. The same flight-hour can be counted only once for Crewmembers' Flight Pay.

Rates: Recipients of Crewmembers' Flight Pay get a monthly payment based on rank. The number of hours of flight don't affect the rate, as long as the monthly time-in-flight requirements are met. The rates in effect for 1997 are as follows:

Rank	*Rate*
E-1	$110
E-2	110
E-3	110
E-4	125
E-5	150
E-6	175
E-7	200
E-8	200
E-9	200
W-1	125
W-2	150
W-3	175
W-4	250
W-5	250
0-1	125
0-2	150
0-3	175
0-4	225
0-5	250
0-6	250
0-7 & Higher	110

These rates change infrequently.

NON-CREWMEMBERS' FLIGHT PAY

People who aren't assigned to an aircraft or to flight duties may find themselves subject to, in the language of federal law, "frequent and regular participation in aerial flight, not as a crew member."

Eligibility: Reserve-component members can qualify while on extended active duty, during other kinds of active duty, and while on inactive-duty status.

Recipients must be aboard a military aircraft in flight during a calendar month to qualify. The number of flight-hours per month isn't a factor in determining eligibility for this kind of flight pay. One flight—of any duration—per month ensures payment of a full month's bonus.

The services have considerable flexibility in deciding who receives this payment. It isn't for servicemembers who fly a lot.

Rates: Active-duty recipients get $110 a month.

Reservists and National Guard members are eligible for one-thirtieth the rate—$3.67—for each official drill period for which they qualify while on inactive-duty or drill status. A typical training day has two drill periods.

This rate goes many years without changing.

Restrictions: Recipients of other flight-related pays, such as ACIP, Crewmembers' Flight Pay, and AWACS pay are ineligible for Non-Crewmembers' Flight Pay.

AWACS FLIGHT PAY

People assigned to Airborne Warning and Control Systems (AWACS) aircraft have their own kind of flight pay. Reservists and National Guardsmen are eligible.

Eligibility: All military members can qualify for this special category of flight pay, whether on active duty or inactive-duty status, as long as they are assigned to AWACS aircraft and take part in regular aerial operations.

Not eligible for this extra pay are military people who fly aboard AWACS aircraft while not crewmembers or those who are eligible for ACIP, Crewmembers' Flight Pay, or Non-Crewmembers' Flight Pay.

Rates: AWACS Flight Pay is a monthly addition to the military paycheck. Amounts are determined by two factors—rank and the number of years of service as an air-weapons controller.

Maximum rates range from $110 a month for a general or admiral with over twenty-five years as an AWACS crew member to $350 a month for mid-career O-3s, O-4s, O-5s and O-6s with less than six years aboard AWACS planes.

Any reserve-component members who qualify for AWACS Flight Pay would receive one-thirtieth of the monthly rate appropriate for their rank and years in AWACS for each drill period in which they flew. Typically, a training day consists of two drill periods.

11

Navy Pays

In This Chapter:

- *Sea Pay*
- *Submarine Pay*
- *Officers' Nuclear Pay*
- *Flight Deck Pay*
- *Commander's Responsibility Pay*

A variety of financial incentives are available to solve specific manpower problems within the sea services. Most of them involve active-duty members, but people in the reserve components can qualify for these Navy pays.

One clarification is important. Although this chapter's title is "Navy Pays," these bonuses are also available to Marines and members of the Coast Guard. In fact, soldiers and airmen can also get these payments if they meet the eligibility requirements.

SEA PAY

Most military members serving aboard naval vessels can receive substantial additions to their monthly paychecks to make up for some of the hazards and hardships of shipboard service. Members of the reserve components can receive Sea Pay as long as they meet the eligibility requirements.

Eligibility: Only recipients of Basic Pay can receive Sea Pay. The kind of active duty being served—extended active duty versus annual training duty, for example—isn't important.

Ineligible for Sea Pay are reservists on inactive-duty status, such as those drawing Drill Pay, or those who agree to come on active duty without pay.

Other eligibility rules for Sea Pay are stringent:

• E-1s, E-2s, and E-3s are ineligible.

• Officers with less than thirty-six months of sea duty are ineligible.

• All recipients must be assigned to a ship, a ship-based staff, or a ship-based aviation unit.

Rates: Sea Pay is a monthly addition to the paychecks of eligible servicemembers. Amounts are set by charts that show a servicemember's rank and number of years of accumulated sea duty.

The enlisted charts start at $50 a month for an E-4 with less than one year's sea duty, and they peak at $520 a month for an E-9 with over sixteen years of sea duty.

For warrant officers, the rates range from $130 a month for a W-1 with less than a year's sea duty to $500 a month for a W-4 with more than eighteen years' sea duty.

For commissioned officers, the rates begin at a $150 a month for O-1s, O-2s, and O-3s with more than three years' sea duty. The top rate for commissioned officers is $380 a month for O-6s.

Sea Pay Premium: In addition to regular Sea Pay, some servicemembers are eligible for a monthly payment for consecutive months of sea duty ("consecutive" is the key word).

Called the Sea Pay Premium, it's $100 a month (1997 rate) for all military members. It begins between the thirty-seventh and sixty-first consecutive month of sea duty depending on rank.

Because of the requirement for consecutive months of sea

duty, only reservists on long stretches of extended active duty are eligible.

SUBMARINE PAY

Members of "the silent service" have their own financial incentives. Submarine Pay is technically known as Incentive Pay for Operational Submarine Duty. A second kind of pay discussed in this section is called Submarine Continuation Pay, although it's technical name is Continuous Monthly Submarine Duty Incentive Pay.

Eligibility: Reserve-component members can qualify for Submarine Pay whether they are on extended active duty, annual training duty, or inactive duty.

Reservists qualifying for Submarine Pay during drill periods or comparable training must serve aboard those vessels while they are under way in order to receive the extra money.

Most recipients of Submarine Pay are submarine crew members. Some shore-based personnel qualify while assigned to submarine headquarters.

Rates: Submarine Pay is a monthly addition to military paychecks. Amounts are based on rank and time in the military. Rates are shown in charts identical in format to the Basic Pay charts.

Reservists on inactive-duty status or on active duty for short periods receive one-thirtieth the monthly rate for each day aboard a vessel in operations.

In 1997, enlisted rates ranged from $75 a month for all E-1s to $355 a month for an E-9 with more than sixteen years of service.

For all warrant officers, the lowest rate was $310 for those with less than two years' service; the top rate of $355 applied to those with more than two years.

Among commissioned officers, O-1s received $175 a month for the first ten years of service, and O-4s qualified for $595 a month after six years.

Submarine Continuation Pay: Servicemembers who are qualified as submariners can continue to receive Submarine Pay even when they're not currently assigned to a submarine or to a submarine staff.

Generally, they must have spent at least six of their first twelve years in the military as qualified submariners.

Reservists on extended active duty can qualify for Submarine Continuation Pay. Reservists on shorter periods of active duty or on inactive-duty status are ineligible.

The rates for Submarine Continuation Pay are the same as those for Submarine Pay. It stops when submariners receive Submarine Pay.

OFFICERS' NUCLEAR PAY

Officers who are qualified to oversee nuclear propulsion systems are eligible for four different sign-up programs. Two are financial incentives to draw officers into the field, and two are bonuses to keep them on active duty.

Eligibility: Reserve-component members must take on substantial active-duty commitments to qualify. Reservists on inactive-duty status are ineligible.

Active-duty recipients who leave full-time service to enter the reserves before finishing their obligations must repay the government part of their bonuses.

> Sign-up bonuses for enlisted people in the nuclear field ended in 1975.

Navy officials have considerable latitude in picking people to become nuclear-qualified officers.

Programs: The four sign-up programs for nuclear-qualified officers are:

Nuclear Officer Accession Bonus: One-time payment of $4,000 for officers with less than five years' commissioned time.

Nuclear Career Accession Bonus: One-time payment of $2,000 to unrestricted-line officers.

Nuclear Continuation Pay: Maximum annual payment of $10,000 for those with at least three years within the nuclear field.

Annual Incentive Bonus: Annual bonus of $7,200 to unrestricted-line officers and $3,600 to limited-duty officers.

FLIGHT DECK PAY

The military has long had a special payment for the men and women whose jobs take them to the flight decks of aircraft carriers. Flight Deck Pay is classified by the military as a hazardous-duty incentive pay, covered by the same general rules as pays listed in Chapter 8.

Eligibility: Reserve-component members can qualify for Flight Deck Pay while on extended active duty, during shorter periods of active duty, and while on inactive-duty status.

Recipients must be:

- Assigned to the crew of an aircraft carrier.
- Required to be on the flight deck during fixed-wing landings and takeoffs.
- Involved four days a month in takeoffs and landings.

The rule about four takeoffs a month doesn't apply to reservists on inactive-duty status. People aboard helicopter-carrying vessels don't qualify.

Military members on temporary duty with aviation units or aircraft carriers can qualify for Flight Deck Pay if they are ordered to serve in a job normally designated for the extra money.

Rates: The rate for Flight Deck Pay is $110 a month. This rate applies equally to officers and enlisted members in the active-duty force and reservists on extended active duty.

Reservists serving at least thirty days on active duty receive the full monthly rate for each calendar month in which they spend at least one day in an eligible position.

Reservists ordered to active duty for less than thirty days

receive one-thirtieth the monthly rate—$3.67—for each day of a calendar month they qualify for the bonus.

Double-Pay Restrictions: Recipients of Flight Deck Pay can receive, simultaneously, Hostile Fire Pay or Imminent Danger Pay. However, they cannot receive for the same calendar month any other kind of extra pay that the military officially categorizes as Hostile Fire Incentive Pay. Those pays are listed in Chapter 8.

COMMANDER'S RESPONSIBILITY PAY

For decades, the Navy and Coast Guard have offered an extra monthly payment for officers in command assignments. Its formal name is Special Pay for Officers Serving in Positions of Unusual Responsibility and of a Critical Nature, but most people know it simply as Responsibility Pay.

Eligibility: Recipients of Responsibility Pay must also receive Basic Pay. That renders ineligible reservists on inactive-duty status, such as those participating in weekend drills or comparable training.

Reservists on all kinds of active duty are, technically, eligible, but other rules—principally that recipients be permanently assigned to a position designated for the extra pay—make it unlikely that reservists on short active-duty stints would qualify.

Rates: Responsibility Pay is a monthly addition to the paychecks of eligible servicemembers. Rates are based strictly on rank, as follows:

- O-3, $ 50
- O-4, $ 50
- O-5, $100
- O-6, $150

If the rates seem like an ungenerous way to compensate people for the extra burdens of command, there's a reason. These were the rates in effect when the bonus was created in 1958.

12

MEDICAL PAYS

In This Chapter:

- *Loan Forgiveness*
- *Selected Reserves Pay*
- *Call-up Bonuses*

People in the reserves and National Guard have skills that span the spectrum of jobs performed by the U.S. armed forces. Not the least of their contributions involves the healing arts.

For health-care professionals, the military has an intricate package of bonuses. Some are token financial recognition for sacrifices; others are hard-nosed incentives to ensure that the armed forces have the right mix of medical professionals.

LOAN FORGIVENESS

Professionals with health-care credentials who enter the reserves or National Guard with student loans may be eligible to have the military pay off those debts.

Eligibility: There are four major eligibility requirements:

- Only commissioned officers qualify.
- The officer must be in a medical field that the military recognizes as a critical wartime specialty.

• The officer must agree to serve in the Selected Reserve, which includes people in reserve-component units and in the manpower pool known as the Individual Mobilization Augmentation (IMA) program.

• The loan must have been used to pay for education in a specialty that the military considers critical.

Not eligible for this program are reservists and National Guard members who were already serving with a reserve-component unit or as an IMA participant when they took out their student loans.

Reserve-component members can also lose their eligibility for this program if they come on active duty for extended periods. Shorter periods of full-time service, such as annual active duty for training, have no effect on eligibility.

Rates: Up to $3,000 in loans can be forgiven for each year that a qualified officer agrees to spend in the reserves or National Guard. There's a lifetime limit of $20,000.

SELECTED RESERVES PAY

The military needs trained professionals in the medical units of the reserve components that help active-duty units. Since 1995, the military has offered a bonus to keep certain medical specialists in the reserves and National Guard. It's known as Special Pay for Selected Reserve Health-Care Professionals.

Eligibility: Only officers are eligible. They must be members of the Selected Reserve, which includes drilling reservists assigned to units, people on full-time unit support, officers who had taken some professionally related courses before entering the military, and members of the Individual Mobilization Augmentation (IMA) program.

Not all medical specialties are covered. The services pick the specialties for which the bonus will be offered. By law, they must be "critically short wartime specialties."

Recipients must sign a contract to spend at least one year in the Selected Reserve. They can commit to as much as three years.

Rates: Participants in qualifying specialties can receive a maximum of $10,000 annually for each year of their commitment.

Payment is made in a lump-sum bonus at the start of each year under the contract. The services can offer amounts less than $10,000.

Repayment: Recipients who lose their professional qualifications or who leave the Selected Reserve must repay the bonus. The repayment formula is tough. Serving anything less than a complete year requires repayment of the full bonus paid for that year.

Because this is a bonus to keep health-care professionals on inactive-duty status, going on full-time active duty also breaks the contract. Those who make the switch may have to repay the government.

CALL-UP BONUSES

A complex array of bonuses is available to health-care professionals in the reserve components who come on active duty for short periods. With a few exceptions, these are the same bonuses that the military offers for extended active duty.

Eligibility: These bonuses go to reservists and National Guard members during specific kinds of call-ups:

- Recalled to active duty for an officially declared national emergency (the call-up must last longer than thirty days but less than one year)
- Retained involuntarily on active duty during a national emergency
- Volunteered to remain on active duty for less than a year during a national emergency when people are being retained involuntarily

> Mobilized health-care professionals can receive many of the financial incentives offered to active-duty doctors and nurses.

Ineligible for call-up bonuses are reserve-component members on active duty for training, even when that occurs during a time when others qualify for this extra money.

Doctors: Four different kinds of bonuses are on the books for physicians during call-ups, each designed to solve a particular personnel shortage or to correct a financial injustice.

Variable Special Pay: Available to most medical officers of the Army, Navy, and Air Force. Rates range from $100 a month for interns to a top rate of $1,000 a month.

Board-Certified Pay: Given to physicians who've passed special examinations within their medical fields. Rates are from $200 a month for people with less than ten years as doctors to $500 a month for those with more than eighteen years' experience.

Additional Special Pay: An incentive for military doctors nearing the end of their obligated time in uniform. All recipients get an additional $1,250 a year.

Incentive Special Pay: Extra money for physicians in critical specialties or for doctors who are isolated geographically. The services can offer a maximum payment of $3,000 a month, although smaller amounts can be given.

A fifth bonus for active-duty physicians, Multi-year Special Pay, isn't offered to call-up doctors. It goes only to professionals who commit to more than a year on active duty.

Dentists: Three different bonuses are available to dentists called up for national emergencies.

Variable Special Pay: Available to most dental officers of the Army, Navy, and Air Force. The pay is between $100 and $500 a month, depending on one's time as a dentist.

Board-Certified Pay: Given to dentists who've passed examinations within their specialties. The rates start at $166 a month for those with less than twelve years as dentists and peak at $333 a month for those with at least fourteen years' experience.

Additional Special Pay: Paid to military dentists with at least three years as dentists. Monthly payments range from $500 for those with less than fourteen years of dental experience to $833 for those with eighteen years or more.

Psychologists: Officers serving on active duty as psychologists can qualify for a monthly payment of $166 to $416, depending on their time in the specialty.

Registered Nurses: Reserve-component nurses who come on active duty for at least four years can receive a one-time bonus of $5,000 (1997 rate).

Reserve and National Guard nurses on active duty for shorter periods, or those recalled to active duty for national emergencies, are ineligible.

Nurse-Anesthetists: Officers who meet the professional standards of nurse-anesthetists and who are assigned to those positions by the military can receive a monthly payment of $500 during emergency call-ups.

Non-Physician Health-Care Providers: A select group of officers who aren't doctors, dentists, or nurses can qualify for a special monthly payment if they're in a medically related field approved by their service for extra money.

Recipients are paid between $166 and $416 a month, depending on their time in their professional fields. Reserve-component members called up for national emergencies can receive this money, as can professionals on extended active duty or other full-time service.

Veterinarians: Professional veterinarians on active duty are entitled to a special payment of $100 a month, whether on extended active duty or called up for a national emergency.

PART III

Living Allowances

13

OVERSEAS PAYS

In This Chapter:

- *Foreign Duty Pay*
- *Overseas Extension Pay*
- *Family Separation Allowances*
- *Overseas Cost-of-Living Allowance*

Being a reservist or a National Guardsman can be an international job. No longer can part-time servicemembers count on spending their time at the neighborhood armory or at the nearest military base for annual training.

Members of the reserve components can be assigned anywhere in the world, even without coming on extended active duty. Whenever assignments take them outside the United States, they may be eligible for the same overseas pays that go to people permanently stationed in foreign nations.

FOREIGN DUTY PAY

Military people in some overseas locations are eligible for a token financial payment for their inconveniences. Reservists can qualify, although those not on extended active duty may find it difficult.

Eligibility: Only enlisted members on active duty are eligible for Foreign Duty Pay.

Reservists and guard members must be assigned on temporary duty to a qualifying location for at least eight days.

People on inactive-duty status are ineligible, as are commissioned officers, warrant officers, and military members drawing Sea Pay.

This extra money goes to military people serving outside the forty-eight contiguous states and the District of Columbia. Not all foreign service qualifies. The military designates the countries—and even the regions within countries—where Foreign Duty Pay will be given.

Rates: Military personnel who qualify for Foreign Duty Pay receive it at rates based solely on their ranks. Rates in effect in 1997 are as follows:

Rank	*Rate*
E-1	$ 8.00
E-2	8.00
E-3	9.00
E-4	13.00
E-5	16.00
E-6	20.00
E-7	22.50
E-8	22.50
E-9	22.50

Foreign Duty Pay is usually paid in a monthly lump sum. It is also known as "Certain Places Pay."

OVERSEAS EXTENSION PAY

Since the early 1980s, Overseas Extension Pay has been given to military people who volunteer to stay longer in a foreign assignment.

Eligibility: Only enlisted personnel are eligible for Overseas Extension Pay. Commissioned officers and warrant officers are ineligible.

Reserve-component members on extended active duty qualify. Reservists and National Guard members on shorter periods of active duty and on inactive-duty status are ineligible.

Recipients must be stationed outside the United States, serve a normal tour, and agree to stay at least one more year.

Rates: All recipients receive either $80 a month or fifteen to thirty days of leave that's not counted toward the annual limit of thirty days' leave.

FAMILY SEPARATION ALLOWANCES

When military members must maintain two households—one for themselves and one for their families—the Family Separation Allowance (FSA) can provide additional money to offset some of the expenses.

General Eligibility: Reserve-component members on extended active duty can qualify for FSA under the same rules as other full-time members of the military.

Reservists and National Guard members on other kinds of active duty are technically eligible to receive the money, but few meet all the eligibility rules.

Ineligible are members of the reserve components on inactive-duty status.

There are two types of Family Separation Allowances. Type I is the more generous program, but type II is much more common. Each has its own eligibility rules.

FSA Type I Eligibility: Servicemembers must meet four major requirements to get this extra payment:

• Recipients are permanently stationed someplace other than Hawaii, the forty-eight contiguous states, or the District of Columbia.

- The government refuses to pay to move family members to the new assignment.
- Family members do not move to the new assignment.
- Government quarters are not available for the military member at the assignment.

FSA Type II Eligibility: The military member must fit into one of three categories:

FSA-R: Dependents are not authorized government-paid travel to the new assignment.

FSA-S: The military member is on shipboard duty away from home port for more than thirty consecutive days.

FSA-T: The military member is on temporary duty for more than thirty days and dependents don't live near the temporary duty assignment.

Dual Eligibility: Everyone receiving type I FSA should also receive the FSA-R type II allowance.

No one can receive two different kinds of type II payment for the same calendar month, however, even if they fit into more than one of the three basic categories.

Rates: Recipients of type I benefits receive their normal Basic Allowance for Quarters at the with-dependents rate, plus an additional monthly BAQ payment computed at the without-dependents rate.

Recipients of type II benefits receive a flat rate of $75 a month (1997 rate). This amount is unaffected by rank, family size, or any other factor.

OVERSEAS COST-OF-LIVING ALLOWANCE

When a military paycheck is spent overseas, it doesn't always have the same purchasing power it has in the States. The Overseas Cost-of-Living Allowance (COLA) was designed to help balance the financial scales.

Eligibility: Reserve-component members on extended

active duty can qualify for the Overseas COLA under the same rules as other full-time members of the military.

Also qualifying are reservists and National Guard members on shorter stints of active duty who are permanently stationed at a qualifying overseas location for at least twenty weeks. Members of the reserve component on inactive-duty status are ineligible.

Most reserve-component recipients of overseas pays are on extended active duty.

Not all countries, and not all locations within the same country, qualify servicemembers for the Overseas COLA.

Rates: Amounts paid for the Overseas COLA can range from a few dollars to several hundred dollars a month.

The actual amount going to an individual is set by a complex formula that includes total military income, the number of dependents, and the Pentagon's official assessment of the overall cost of goods and services in a foreign community.

14

HOUSING ALLOWANCES

In This Chapter:

- *Variable Housing Allowance*
- *Overseas Housing Allowance*
- *Utility / Recurring Maintenance Allowance*
- *Stateside Cost-of-Living Allowance*

The housing allowances paid to military members have two crystal-clear points for members of the reserve components. First, those on extended active duty are eligible for housing allowances under the same rules as the full-time force. Second, those on inactive-duty status are ineligible for housing allowances.

There is also a murky area, typically involving reservists and guardsmen on short stints of active duty. This chapter explores some of those fuzzy regions in the regulations. (Keep in mind that the bedrock of housing allowances, the Basic Allowance for Quarters, is discussed in Chapter 3.)

VARIABLE HOUSING ALLOWANCE

For members of the full-time military living off base within the United States, the primary paycheck addition that can help with housing costs is the Variable Housing Allowance (VHA).

Eligibility: Those on extended active duty are covered by the same rules that apply to everyone else on active duty, and those on inactive-duty status are ineligible for VHA.

Here's how the rules apply to reserve-component members who come on active duty for specific short periods of time:

Ordered to active duty for at least twenty weeks: These people are eligible for VHA from the moment they qualify for BAQ, which is usually the first formal day on active duty. They receive VHA at the rate appropriate for their duty stations. Between the time they come on active duty and the time they report at those duty stations, they can be paid VHA at the rate appropriate for their hometowns.

Ordered to active duty for less than twenty weeks: These people are usually not eligible for VHA, unless the recall was for a national emergency or a possible wartime operation.

Ordered to active duty for a contingency operation: These people are eligible for VHA from the first day on active duty, using rates in effect for the servicemember's hometown. Included are single reservists and guard members who are buying their own homes or who must keep their apartments.

Receiving Incapacitation Pay: These members are eligible for VHA while receiving Incapacitation Pay and recovering from injuries incurred on active duty or during inactive-duty training. The rate is based on the servicemember's hometown, and the maximum duration is six months.

Note that reservists on their two-week active-duty stints for annual training don't qualify for VHA.

Whether on full-time duty or short periods of active duty, reserve-component members must also meet a number of other eligibility criteria to qualify for VHA.

The area—either duty station or hometown—on which VHA rates are based must be one for which the military has approved VHA. Not all communities are authorized VHA, nor are all ranks within the same community.

Rates: VHA rates are personalized. The Defense Department establishes rates in each stateside civilian community for military members at each rank and, within each rank, for those with dependents and those without dependents.

The rates can range from hundreds of dollars to a few dollars. For many military folks living in civilian communities, the rate is zero.

Actually, the rates are maximums. To get the maximum rate, military people must be able to show that their housing expenses are greater than their VHA plus their BAQ. If their expenses are less than the two housing allowances added together, the government withholds some of the excess payment.

OVERSEAS HOUSING ALLOWANCE

For full-time members of the military living off base outside the United States, the primary paycheck addition that can help with housing costs is the Overseas Housing Allowance (OHA).

Eligibility: Reservists and National Guard members on extended active duty are covered by the same rules that apply to everyone else on active duty. Reserve-component members on inactive-duty status are ineligible for OHA.

Reserve-component members who come on active duty for at least twenty weeks and who are permanently stationed overseas are eligible. Those on active duty for less than twenty weeks are generally ineligible for OHA.

Under the rules for OHA, recipients must be authorized by their commanders to live in off-base communities. Eligibility isn't affected by whether military members have dependents living with them, although that does affect rates.

Rates: The Defense Department has OHA rates for each overseas off-base community where U.S. military people tend to live. At each location, there is a separate rate for each rank and, within each rank, for those with dependents and those without dependents.

OHA rates are actually maximums. Many OHA recipients receive less than the top rate if their housing expenses are low. An individual's actual rate is determined by a complex formula that includes local housing costs, other military housing-related payments, and the servicemember's actual expenses.

OHA rates are subject to review by the military. Normally, they change twice a year. If rates go down, OHA recipients find themselves getting less money to meet their expenses.

UTILITY/RECURRING MAINTENANCE ALLOWANCE

Most OHA recipients also receive a second, separate payment called the Utility/Maintenance Allowance. It's designed to compensate them for the cost of their utilities.

Eligibility: Technically, everyone receiving OHA qualifies for the Utility/Maintenance Allowance. Whether a person actually receives it is determined by the individual's housing costs.

Rates: Like the overall OHA rate, this allowance is customized by overseas location. Unlike OHA, the Utility/Maintenance Allowance doesn't have separate rates for each rank.

STATESIDE COST-OF-LIVING ALLOWANCE

Since 1995, military members assigned to unusually high-cost areas within the forty-eight contiguous states have been eligible for a bonus to make up for the extra expense. It's called the Stateside Cost-of-Living Allowance (COLA) or the CONUS COLA (short for continental U.S.).

Eligibility: Reserve-component members on extended active duty are eligible under the same rules as the full-time military. People on inactive-duty status are ineligible.

Here's how the eligibility rules apply to reservists and guardsmen on short active-duty stints:

Ordered to active duty for at least twenty weeks: These

members are eligible for Stateside COLA from the moment they qualify for BAQ, which is usually the first formal day on active duty. They receive the bonus at the rate appropriate for their duty stations. Between the time they come on active duty and the time they report at those duty stations, they can be paid Stateside COLA at the rate appropriate for their hometowns.

Ordered to active duty for less than twenty weeks: These people are usually not eligible for Stateside COLA, unless the recall was for a national emergency or a possible wartime operation.

Ordered to active duty for a contingency operation: These members are eligible for Stateside COLA from the first day on active duty, using rates in effect for the servicemember's hometown. Included are single reservists and guard members who are buying their own homes or who must keep their apartments.

Mobilized reservists may qualify for the new CONUS COLA.

Note that reservists on their two-week active-duty stints for annual training don't qualify for the Stateside COLA because they're on active duty for less than 20 weeks.

Whether on extended active duty or on full-time service for short periods of time, reserve-component members must also meet the other eligibility rules for Stateside COLA.

The area on which Stateside COLA is based—either duty station or hometown—must be one for which the military has approved Stateside COLA. Few communities are authorized this bonus.

Rates: Stateside COLA amounts are based on rank, whether a person has dependents, and the location—either the duty station or the dependents' home—used for eligibility.

In 1997, the rates ranged from about $10 to nearly $500 a month.

15

MOVING PAYMENTS

In This Chapter:

- *Overview on Eligibility*
- *Household Goods Weight Allowance*
- *Government-Paid Storage*
- *Move-in Housing Allowance*
- *Dislocation Allowance*
- *Temporary Lodging (Stateside)*
- *Temporary Lodging (Overseas)*
- *Mileage Allowance and Per Diem (Member)*
- *Mileage Allowance and Per Diem (Dependents)*
- *Government-Paid Transportation*

The dividing line between full-time military members and part-timers such as reservists and National Guard members is easiest to see when it comes to moving. Government-ordered moves are a fact of life for active-duty personnel. For members of the reserve components, they're rare. Still, there are times when reservists and National Guardsmen have to pay attention to the fine print in the travel regulations.

OVERVIEW ON ELIGIBILITY

For most of the reassignment-related programs, reservists and National Guard members fall into three basic eligibility groups:

Extended Active Duty: Reservists and National Guard members on extended active duty are treated the same way as other full-time servicemembers who are given orders that call for a permanent change of station (PCS).

Usually, reserve-component members must be brought on active duty for at least twenty consecutive months in one location to qualify for government-paid moves.

Short Active-Duty Periods: Reservists and guard members coming on active duty for less than twenty weeks qualify for limited benefits. These limited benefits also apply to those reporting for their two weeks of annual active-duty training and to those people on active duty for what's officially classified as initial active duty for training.

Inactive-Duty Status: Reserve-component members on inactive-duty status—that is, those drawing Drill Pay, taking part in weekend drill periods, or undergoing comparable training—cannot receive reassignment-related benefits from the military. This prohibition extends to people whose reserve-component units move to another area.

HOUSEHOLD GOODS WEIGHT ALLOWANCE

The Household Goods Weight Allowance is a rank-by-rank listing of the weight of personal property that the government will pay to move when people are reassigned (see the accompanying box).

Eligibility: See "Overview on Eligibility" at the beginning of this chapter.

Stateside PCS Moves: When people are transferred by the military to a new assignment officially classified as a permanent change of station, the government will pick up the costs of moving their household property.

HOUSEHOLD GOODS WEIGHT ALLOWANCE (1997)

Rank	*With Dependents*	*Without Dependents*
O-6 & higher	18,000	18,000
O-5 & W-5	17,500	16,000
O-4 & W-4	17,000	14,000
O-3 & W-3	14,500	13,000
O-2 & W-2	13,500	12,500
O-1 & W-1	12,000	10,000
E-9	14,500	12,000
E-8	13,500	11,000
E-7	12,500	10,500
E-6	11,000	8,000
E-5	9,000	7,000
E-4 (more than 2 years)	8,000	7,000
E-4 (2 years or less)	7,000	3,500
E-3	5,000	2,000
E-2	5,000	1,500
E-1	5,000	1,500

Qualifying under these rules are reserve-component members on extended active duty, those brought on active duty for at least twenty weeks in one location, and those with an initial stretch of active duty lasting more than six months.

Overseas PCS Moves: For overseas moves, the amount of personal property that the government will pay to move is set on a country-by-country basis. Usually, it's 2,000 pounds for a family or 25 percent of a servicemember's Household Weight Allowance, whichever is larger.

Temporary Moves: Reservists on active duty for less than twenty weeks, plus active-duty personnel with written orders

TEMPORARY ASSIGNMENT WEIGHT ALLOWANCE (1997)

Rank	*Weight*
O-10	2,000
O-9	1,500
O-8	1,000
O-7	1,000
O-6	800
O-5 & W-5	800
O-4 & W-4	800
O-3 & W-3	600
O-2 & W-2	600
O-1 & W-1	600
E-9	600
E-8	500
E-7	400
E-6	400
E-5	400
E-4 (more than 2 years)	400
E-4 (2 years or less)	225
E-3	225
E-2	225
E-1	225

for temporary duty or temporary additional duty, have their own weight chart for personal property (see the accompanying box). These weight limits are supposed to represent the weight of unpacked, uncrated personal property.

GOVERNMENT-PAID STORAGE

For a variety of personal reasons, military families who are shipping their household goods may want the delivery of some or all of their property delayed. For them, there is government-paid storage.

Eligibility: Anyone entitled to a government-paid shipment of household goods is entitled to government-paid storage.

When reservists and National Guard members are called to active duty for a national emergency or a deployment, they're eligible for government-paid storage of their personal goods, using the full household goods weight allowance. The duration of the recall—whether it's more or less than twenty weeks—is irrelevant, although the reason for the recall must be a national emergency or a deployment.

Thirty days of government-paid storage is authorized after a reserve-component member is discharged from active duty if the reservist or guardsman was on active duty for:

- Initial active duty for training for less than six months
- Active duty—including annual active-duty training—for less than twenty weeks
- Active duty for more than twenty weeks, but with less than twenty weeks spent in any single location

Reservists leaving active duty after longer periods are usually authorized 180 days of government-paid storage.

Amounts: Everything put in storage is counted against a servicemember's official weight allowance.

For example, an active-duty E-5 with dependents is authorized 9,000 pounds of property for the full household goods weight allowance. If that E-5 moves 7,000 pounds at government expense to a new assignment, the most the government will pay to store is 2,000 pounds.

MOVE-IN HOUSING ALLOWANCE

Establishing a new home overseas can be expensive. The Move-in Housing Allowance (MIHA) comes to the rescue of military people facing these expenses. MIHA is actually three programs—MIHA/Miscellaneous, MIHA/Rent, and MIHA/Security.

Eligibility: See "Overview on Eligibility" at the beginning of this chapter.

Reserve-component members on short periods of active duty must be permanently stationed at an overseas location for at least twenty weeks to qualify. Everyone receiving the OHA is eligible for MIHA.

Some one-time expenses facing renters qualify for reimbursement from the government under MIHA/Rent. Covered expenses include real estate agents' fees, redecoration fees, and one-time lease taxes.

Military personnel assigned to specific countries with a high possibility of attack by terrorists or an unusually high crime rate can qualify under MIHA/Security for reimbursements for security-related improvements to their off-base private homes.

Rates: Each overseas locality that has rates for OHA also has an MIHA/Miscellaneous rate. There's only one MIHA/Miscellaneous rate per locality; unlike OHA, different ranks don't receive different payments.

DISLOCATION ALLOWANCE

To close the gap between the expenses military people face during reassignments and the government's reimbursements, the military offers the Dislocation Allowance.

Eligibility: See "Overview on Eligibility" at the beginning of this chapter.

Whether a reserve-component member or an active-duty person, recipients of the Dislocation Allowance must have what the military calls a permanent-change-of-station (PCS) move.

People with family members who qualify as dependents always receive this allowance. Those without dependents receive the Dislocation Allowance only if they're not assigned to government quarters at their new location.

Rates: The Dislocation Allowance is equal to two months' BAQ.

As a rule, military personnel can receive only one payment of the Dislocation Allowance per fiscal year.

TEMPORARY LODGING (STATESIDE)

People reassigned within the States are often eligible for the Temporary Lodging Expense (TLE) to help defray the costs of living in hotels, motels, or other temporary housing.

Eligibility: See "Overview on Eligibility" at the beginning of this chapter.

TLE recipients must undergo a PCS move in the States for which they have temporary lodging costs not covered by other travel benefits, especially per diem.

Family members who meet the official definition of dependent can receive this allowance for expenses while traveling separately from the military member.

Rates: The maximum TLE payment is $110 a day. This is not a guaranteed payment. The amount a person receives is determined by a complex formula that includes the number of people traveling together, the local per diem rate, actual housing expenses, and the facilities available in the hotel or motel.

Duration: For servicemembers transferred from one stateside assignment to another, TLE benefits last a maximum of ten days. Ten days is also the limit for people reassigned to the States from an overseas post. For permanent transfers from the States to a location overseas, the maximum duration of TLE payments is five days.

TEMPORARY LODGING (OVERSEAS)

Military members reassigned overseas are frequently eligible for the Temporary Lodging Allowance (TLA) to help defray the costs of living in temporary civilian quarters and eating meals "on the economy."

Eligibility: See "Overview on Eligibility" at the beginning of this chapter.

Generally, TLA recipients have either arrived at a new duty station overseas where government quarters aren't available for immediate occupancy, or they've left their permanent housing overseas and haven't begun traveling to a new assignment.

Family members who are classified as dependents can qualify for TLA payments under some circumstances when the servicemember is no longer overseas.

Rates: Technically, there's no maximum TLA payment.

The amount that any individual receives is determined by a formula that includes the local per diem rate and the servicemember's actual expenses for temporary housing.

MILEAGE ALLOWANCE AND PER DIEM (MEMBER)

A single benefit pays many relocation costs for reassigned military members, their families, and the family car. Called MALT-Plus (for Monetary Allowance in Lieu of Transportation), it's a combination of mileage allowance and per diem.

Eligibility: See "Overview on Eligibility" at the beginning of this chapter.

> Being reassigned to a new unit for drill periods doesn't make a servicemember eligible for a government-paid move.

Ineligible are reserve-component members traveling as a group in government-provided transportation, plus reservists and guardsmen whose active-duty assignments are within commuting distance of their pre-call-up homes. Also ineligible are reservists and National Guard members who are on inactive-duty status and are assigned to new units.

Mileage Rates: Military people eligible for a mileage allowance as part of a PCS move receive the following rates for the military member and official dependents:

- 15 cents for one traveler
- 17 cents for two travelers
- 19 cents for three travelers
- 20 cents for four or more travelers

Slightly higher rates are in effect for reservists and guard members coming on active duty for less than twenty weeks. This includes people traveling to the sites of their annual active-duty-for-training stints. Their rates are pegged to the mode of transportation. In 1997, the per-mile rates were:

- 31 cents by automobile
- 25 cents by motorcycle
- 85 cents by privately owned airplane

Reservists and National Guard members who have been recalled to active duty—for whatever duration—and who are able to commute from their original homes to their official duty stations qualify for a mileage allowance of 30 cents per mile for one round-trip daily.

Per Diem Rates: Most military members entitled to a mileage allowance while making a PCS move are also entitled to a per diem. It's a flat rate of $50 a day (1997 rate). Keeping receipts is not required, since the per diem is the same regardless of actual costs.

Reservists and National Guard members who have been recalled to active duty—for whatever duration—and who are able to commute from their original homes to their official duty stations qualify for government reimbursement for two meals daily. The amount of the reimbursement cannot exceed the daily per diem rate for that community.

MILEAGE ALLOWANCE AND PER DIEM (DEPENDENTS)

In narrowly drawn circumstances, the spouses, children, and other official dependents of active-duty personnel can receive financial help from the government to get themselves from one duty station to another when the military member is reassigned.

Eligibility: See "Overview on Eligibility" at the beginning of this chapter.

The mileage allowance and per diem are usually paid to the families of reservists and National Guard members on extended active duty who are ordered to another assignment.

The mileage allowance, but not the per diem, can be paid to official dependents of reserve-component members brought on active duty for at least twenty weeks in one location.

Families of reserve-component members on active duty for less than twenty weeks in any one location—a category that includes reservists and guardsmen during their annual two-week stints on active duty—are ineligible for either a mileage allowance or a per diem to join the servicemember.

Mileage Rates: Whether traveling alone or with the servicemember, the rates for dependents traveling to a new permanent duty station are the same as for active-duty people:

- 15 cents for one traveler
- 17 cents for two travelers
- 19 cents for three travelers
- 20 cents for four or more travelers

Per Diem Rates: When dependents travel to a new assignment with the active-duty member, each dependent twelve years of age and older is entitled to a per diem of $37.50. For dependents younger than twelve, the rate is $25.

These same rates apply when a solitary dependent travels to a new duty station. When two or more dependents travel together to a new assignment (without the servicemember), one dependent is entitled to a per diem of $50, and each additional dependent receives $37.50 or $25, depending on his or her age.

Vehicles: If the service has authorized travel to a new assignment by private car, usually the military member is automatically entitled to use two family vehicles.

This has an effect on the total mileage allowance. For example, a husband and wife traveling in one car are entitled to 17 cents a mile. In two cars, each is entitled to the one-traveler rate of 15 cents a mile, for a family total of 30 cents a mile in two cars.

Using three or more family cars requires the permission of the official who issued the original reassignment orders.

GOVERNMENT-PAID TRANSPORTATION

When military orders make a servicemember or family members eligible for government-paid airline tickets, train tickets, bus tickets, or passenger liner tickets, some other travel-related expenses may be reimbursed by the military. Reimbursable expenses include:

- Public transportation needed to get to government-provided transportation. This includes taxis, buses, and streetcars. It is applicable only when free transportation is unavailable.
- Tips to train attendants—limit of $1 per day.
- Tips to taxi drivers—limit of 15 percent of fare.
- Costs of obtaining passports, passport photos, birth certificates, and visas.
- Costs of traveler's checks.
- Tips to stewards aboard ship—not to exceed $5 a day for one traveler, $9 for two, $13 for three, $16 for four.

Talk to the staff at the travel office before incurring any large expenses under the assumption that the government will reimburse them.

16

LINE-OF-DUTY PAYMENTS

In This Chapter:

- *Uniform Allowances*
- *Traveling to Annual Training*
- *Extraordinary Travel Expenses*
- *Civilian Clothing Allowances*

Even for members of the reserve components, military service isn't like any other job. The reserves and the National Guard impose far-reaching obligations on their members, and to make up for some of those pressures, the military has some financial benefits that don't have private-sector counterparts.

This chapter provides details about a variety of disparate payments. None of the payments listed in this chapter appear in any official publication as "Line-of-Duty Payments." That phrase is used here for the convenience of new members of the military who are still learning the language.

UNIFORM ALLOWANCES

Typically, reservists and National Guard members receive uniform allowances appropriate for their service—or the actual uniform items themselves—when first coming on active duty for their initial training. Only under specific circumstances do members of the reserve components receive additional uniform allowances or uniform items.

Officers: Reserve and National Guard officers can qualify for uniform allowances on two occasions. Some people qualify for both simultaneously.

Initial: Reserve-component officers receive a onetime $200 uniform allowance after fourteen days on active duty for training or after fourteen drill periods while on inactive duty. This is the same allowance officers receive when going on extended active duty.

If reserve or National Guard officers have previously received the $200 uniform allowance for full-time active duty, they normally cannot qualify for it again by going onto active duty for short periods or onto inactive-duty status.

The only two-time recipients of this allowances are reserve officers who served in one branch of the military—either on active duty or in a reserve component—then switched to another branch of the military. An example of this would be an Army reserve officer transferring to the Air National Guard or to the Navy.

Active duty: Reserve-component officers returning to active duty can qualify for a $100 uniform allowance to bring their wardrobe up to snuff.

Recipients must be ordered to active duty for at least ninety days.

Ineligible are officers who received their initial $200 uniform allowances within the past two years. Also ineligible are those returning to active duty after being away for less than two years, even when those officers didn't receive a $100 uniform maintenance allowance during the earlier tour.

Women-Only Allowances: Enlisted female members of the reserve components may be entitled to a one-time Initial Cash Allowance if they are unable to obtain appropriate underclothing and other personal items through official supply channels when they first come on active duty.

Navy Allowances: Enlisted members of the naval reserve may be eligible for special uniform allowances at two points in their careers.

New E-7s: Enlisted members newly promoted to E-7 are eligible for a one-time uniform allowance to purchase special uniform items. This also applies to E-7s who never received this allowance when assigned to drilling units.

The 1997 rate is about $400. The actual amount varies from year to year. It's set at one-half the amount given to new active-duty E-7s.

E-7s and higher: A quarterly uniform allowance is payable to some members of the naval reserve in the ranks of E-7, E-8, and E-9. Called the Reserve Quarterly Maintenance Clothing Allowance, it goes to senior enlisted members who participate in at least 75 percent of their units' scheduled drill periods.

The quarterly amount is $9. It's paid only to enlisted members who qualify for a full quarter. Fractional payments aren't authorized.

TRAVELING TO ANNUAL TRAINING

When reserve-component members are traveling to and from their annual two-week stints on active duty, they're eligible for one of several financial packages to help defray the costs of travel, food, and sometimes lodging. The financial help depends on the method of travel.

Group Travel: Reserve-component members under orders to travel to an assignment usually aren't eligible for a mileage allowance, a meals allowance, or housing allowances.

In most cases, meals and lodging are provided by the government. Normally, officers must pay for their meals.

If reservists or guard members taking part in group travel

have to pay for housing, the government can reimburse them for reasonable expenses.

When travel orders call for reserve-component members to travel in a group and they end up traveling on their own, they're usually ineligible for any kind of payment for travel expenses, food, or lodging.

Individual Travel: Travel orders may require reservists or National Guard members traveling to an annual training site to obtain a government travel request, or GTR.

A GTR is a voucher that, when handed in at a busline, railroad, or airline, permits the civilian firm to give the servicemember a ticket and to bill the government directly. GTR travelers are eligible for a per diem ranging from $26 to $38 to take care of food and incidental expenses.

Reservists and guard members traveling to active-duty stints using the family car are eligible for a program called Lodging-Plus. It reimburses military members for the costs of renting hotel or motel rooms while on the road.

Each stateside community has a maximum rate for which the government will make lodging reimbursements. If travelers exceed those maximums, the extra money comes from their own pockets.

The "plus" in Lodging-Plus is an allowance for meals. The allowances—known technically as M&IE, for meals and incidental expenses—come in four sizes, depending on the community. They're not affected by actual food expenses. Military members who receive Lodging-Plus get the maximum M&IE per diem for that locality.

The four daily stateside rates (1997) are $30, $34, $38, and $42.

Overseas, the M&IE rates fluctuate significantly, going from a low of $13 a day in many places to more than $200 a day in parts of Japan.

The day that someone leaves home for summer camp and

the day that that person returns aren't automatically days for which the servicemember receives the full per diem amount. Those days are divided into four quarters:

- One minute past midnight to 6 A.M.
- 6:01 A.M. to noon
- One minute past noon to 6 P.M.
- 6:01 P.M. to midnight

For the day of departure and the day of arrival, travelers get one-fourth of the per diem per quarter-day, depending on when their travel started and ended.

EXTRAORDINARY TRAVEL EXPENSES

Not even the U.S. military has enough rules to cover every situation. When it comes to extraordinary expenses for servicemembers traveling on government business, a little-known program that may be of help is called the Actual Expense Allowance.

Eligibility: Reservists and National Guard members are most frequently eligible for this unusual benefit when traveling to missile launchings, world's fairs, national and international sporting events, or natural disasters, where government food and lodging are unavailable and the usual Lodging-Plus rate may be temporarily inadequate.

Rates: The Actual Expense Allowance is a reimbursement with several different maximum payments, depending on circumstances.

CIVILIAN CLOTHING ALLOWANCES

For some military people, the uniform of the day is a civilian suit. Some intelligence personnel and criminal investigators, plus those in foreign areas where the presence of the U.S. military is unwelcome, can be authorized a Civilian Clothing Allowance to pay for duty-hour clothes.

Eligibility: A rarity among reserve-component members, the civilian clothing allowance goes to people with official duties that require them to wear civilian dress. Approval is on a case-by-case basis. Officers are eligible for this allowance only when stationed overseas.

Initial Payments: The amount of the Civilian Clothing Allowance is determined by two factors—the length of the tour for which civilian clothing is needed, and whether the servicemember will need separate sets of clothing for winter and summer.

Rates range from about $500 to more than $1,200. Lesser amounts can be authorized for temporary assignments.

Follow-on Payments: After finishing a tour for which the Civilian Clothing Allowance was made, military people can qualify for a second, reduced payment if they spend more time in that assignment.

The rates for these follow-on payments are as follows:

- Additional six months in assignment, 20 percent
- Additional twelve months in assignment, 30 percent
- Full additional tour, 50 percent

The services have the authority to approve 50 percent of the full allowance for military people who don't qualify under the full-additional-tour rules.

PART IV

BASIC MILITARY BENEFITS

17

HEALTH CARE

In This Chapter:

- *For Members*
- *For Families*

Next to a paycheck, the most important benefit that most people receive from military service is health care. From sick call to the most sophisticated machinery in a modern hospital, the best that the medical world has to offer is provided, free of charge, to the men and women of the U.S. military.

Members of the reserve components, and occasionally their family members, can avail themselves of this important benefit under rules that are fairly straightforward.

FOR MEMBERS

Reserve-component members can receive free medical and dental care. But, like their uniforms, health-care eligibility is sometimes on and sometimes off.

Eligibility: Here are the basic eligibility rules for members of the reserve components during several major points in their military careers:

Active duty: Military people are eligible for full, free medical and dental care, regardless how an injury, illness, or disease is incurred. Full eligibility applies to reserve-component members on active duty for thirty-one days or more.

For reserve-component members on active duty for thirty days or less—which applies to people on two-week stints of active duty—medical care applies only to health problems directly caused or aggravated in the line of duty. Treatment continues, in the words of federal law, until the medical problem "cannot be materially improved by further hospitalization or treatment."

Drill periods: Reservists and National Guard members can receive government-provided medical care if they're injured or they become ill during drill periods.

This medical or dental care continues only until their condition, in the words of federal law, "cannot be materially improved by further hospitalization or treatment."

Also covered under this rule are reservists and guard members injured while traveling to an official drill period or returning home from one.

Some reservists and guardsmen who belong to the Selected Reserve, which includes reserve-component members assigned to units as well as members of the skilled manpower pool known as the Individual Mobilization Augmentation (IMA) program, can purchase dental insurance for themselves from a government-run program called the Selected Reserve Dental Program, which began in 1997.

For this dental coverage, they must pay premiums that are withheld from their military pay. This is a new benefit and was scheduled for tests throughout the late 1990s.

After discharge: Reserve-component members leaving extended active duty can purchase government-backed health insurance under the Continued Health Care Benefit Program. Coverage is in three-month blocks, and it can last for up to eighteen months after discharge.

Reservists and National Guard members leaving active duty after an official "contingency operation" qualify for thirty days of free military medical care after discharge. This thirty-day period ends sooner if the veteran qualifies for an employer-provided health insurance plan.

Reserve-component members getting Incapacitation Pay continue receiving free military medical care until, in the words of federal law, their conditions "cannot be materially improved by further hospitalization or treatment."

Any former member of the military is free at any time to file for VA Disability Compensation (see Chapter 24). If the veteran shows that a medical problem was caused or aggravated by military service, the veteran receives free lifetime treatment in any VA hospital or clinic for that specific medical problem.

Retirement: Reserve-component members who receive military retired pay can seek medical care in any hospital or clinic run by the armed forces. Local medical officials set priorities for treatment and, as a practical matter, military retirees are rarely admitted to on-base health-care facilities.

Reserve-component members receiving military retired pay are also eligible for coverage under the government-backed CHAMPUS health insurance program and the newer Tricare health insurance program. At age sixty-five, all military retirees lose CHAMPUS and Tricare benefits and become eligible for Medicare.

So-called gray-area retirees are *ineligible* for any medical benefits. These reservists and guardsmen have accumulated twenty "good" years but haven't reached their sixtieth birthdays, when reserve-component retirement checks begin.

Like veterans who don't receive retired pay, reserve-component retirees can file at any time for VA Disability Compensation (see Chapter 24). People can qualify for both military retired pay and VA Disability Compensation, but there's one hitch: retirees lose one dollar of retired pay for each dollar of VA money received.

Rates: All medical and dental care provided in a military facility is free. Some people, especially officers, may have to make token payments for food.

Coverage for retirees under CHAMPUS and Tricare involves some out-of-pocket expenses. Following are the major financial features of the programs as they affected retirees in 1997:

CHAMPUS: No enrollment fee, $150 deductible per person or $300 per family (annual out-of-pocket payment) before full coverage begins, $7,500 catastrophic cap (maximum out-of-pocket payment per year). Co-payments (out-of-pocket payments) of 25 percent of bills for visiting civilian doctors, 25 percent of hospitalization charges, 25 percent for prescription medicine. These are the features of standard CHAMPUS; other versions of CHAMPUS have different financial features.

Tricare: Annual enrollment fee of $230 for individual retirees, $460 for families, no deductible, $3,000 catastrophic cap (maximum out-of-pocket payment per year). Co-payments (out-of-pocket payments) of $12 for each doctor visit, $11 a day for hospitalization, $9 for prescription medicine. These are the features of Tricare Prime; like CHAMPUS, Tricare has different versions with different financial features.

Leave: Active-duty people continue to accrue regular leave at the rate of 2.5 days a month even while they are away from their duties because of medical problems.

Reservists and guardsmen must serve on active duty for thirty consecutive days before they get any annual leave. In this case, being officially on active duty for medical treatment is the same as being on active duty for training or full-time duty.

Pay: Reservists and National Guard members on active duty continue receiving Basic Pay, BAQ (if eligible), and BAS (at the appropriate rate) when they are unable to work because of a medical problem.

Some people with protracted medical problems are given orders to make a permanent-change-of-station (PCS) move that officially assigns them to a hospital. PCS orders can affect BAQ and BAS.

> When they're eligible for military health care, reservists and guard members can go to any Department of Defense facility.

In the case of some skill-related pays and hazardous duty pays, the amount of time that people can receive them is limited if medical problems—even problems *caused* by the skill or hazardous duty—make them unable to work. Check the index of *Reservist's Money Guide* for the specific kinds of payments.

Reserve-component members on active duty for periods less than thirty days—which includes those on annual active-duty training—receive their regular active-duty paychecks for periods of illness or injury. However, they're likely to be released from active duty if it appears that they'll be unable perform any work. They should qualify for Incapacitation Pay (see Chapter 24).

Reservists and members of the National Guard on inactive duty, as drill periods are officially called, also receive Drill Pay for any drill periods during which they become ill or are injured. They also may qualify for Incapacitation Pay (see Chapter 24) if they are unable to perform military duties.

Incapacitation Pay also goes to reservists and guardsmen whose ability to perform their regular civilian jobs is affected by a military-related illness or injury.

FOR FAMILIES

At various times, the families of reservists and National Guard members can receive free health care from military facilities or low-cost care in government-backed programs. Spouses, children, and other relatives can also find themselves without any rights to military medical care. It all depends on the status of the military member.

Eligibility: Two factors determine eligibility for free medical and dental care for the families of reserve-component members. These two factors involve the status of the family member and of the military member.

> For family members to qualify for military medical care, servicemembers must be on active duty for at least thirty-one days.

When it comes to family members, people seeking military medical care must meet the armed forces' technical definition of "dependent," which includes:

- Spouses
- Children who haven't reached their twenty-first birthday
- Children who are full-time students and who haven't reached their twenty-third birthday
- Children of any age who are incapable of self support because of disabilities that began before their twenty-first birthday (or twenty-third birthday, in the case of full-time students)
- Parents and parents-in-law who receive at least half their income from the servicemember
- Widows and widowers of military retirees and people who die on active duty
- Ex-spouses who haven't remarried, who were married to the military member for at least twenty years, whose former spouse was credited with at least twenty "good" years, and whose marriage occurred during at least twenty of those "good" years

Children who meet the age limits mentioned above may be legitimate offspring, adopted children, children awaiting adoption by the military family, or stepchildren.

Eligibility for family members also depends on some rules

that involve the person in uniform. Here are the major categories:

Active duty: Families of reservists and National Guard members under orders calling for thirty-one days or more on active duty can receive free medical and dental care in any on-base medical facility.

Eligibility for the family begins on the military member's first day on active duty, not on the thirty-first day.

Family members of qualified reservists and guardsmen on active duty are also eligible for coverage under the military's CHAMPUS and Tricare health insurance systems.

Technically, dependents qualify for on-base dental care on a "space available" basis. As a practical matter, space is rarely available.

Family members of reservists and National Guard members on active duty for periods of thirty days or less are *ineligible* for any government-provided medical care. This means that they don't qualify for military health care when the reservist or guardsman is on active duty for an annual two-week stint for training.

Inactive duty: No free government-provided medical or dental benefits are available to family members of reserve-component members who are on inactive-duty status (that is during weekend drill periods).

As this book went to press, families were ineligible for government-backed dental insurance that was available to some members of the Selected Reserves.

After discharge: Reserve-component members leaving extended active duty can purchase government-backed health insurance for their families under the Continued Health Care Benefit Program. Coverage is in three-month blocks, and it can last for up to eighteen months after discharge.

Reservists and National Guard members leaving active duty after an official "contingency operation" can qualify for thirty days of free military medical care after discharge for their spouses, children, and other dependents. This thirty-day period ends sooner if the veteran qualifies for an employer-provided health insurance plan.

Family members of some discharged veterans can qualify for a CHAMPUS-like program run by the Department of Veterans Affairs. Called CHAMPVA, it's a last-ditch program for dependents who aren't eligible for CHAMPUS or Medicare. Like CHAMPUS and Medicare, CHAMPVA requires participants to pay some out-of-pocket medical expenses.

CHAMPVA participants include:

- Spouses and dependent children of veterans who've been officially classified by VA officials as having a permanent and total service-connected disability
- Spouses and dependent children of veterans who died from a service-connected condition
- Spouses and dependent children of veterans who died while officially rated as having a permanent and total disability
- Spouses and dependent children of veterans who died on active duty

CHAMPVA is a VA program. Details and applications are available from VA medical centers and regional offices.

Retirement: Reserve-component retirees don't begin receiving retired pay until their sixtieth birthday. Until the retired pay begins, family members (along with the reservists or guard members) are ineligible for military medical care, CHAMPUS, or Tricare.

On the reserve-component member's sixtieth birthday, family members also become eligible for on-base medical care, CHAMPUS, and Tricare.

Like all CHAMPUS and Tricare recipients, they must pay some of their costs. They also lose eligibility for those programs when they become eligible for Medicare, usually at their sixty-fifth birthday.

18

Education Payments

In This Chapter:

- *Montgomery GI Bill: Selected Reserves*
- *Montgomery GI Bill: Active Duty*
- *VEAP*

Since the end of World War II, educational benefits have been a major incentive for people to join the military. That's one military tradition that continues today, providing the all-volunteer forces with the right mix of highly educated, highly motivated people in uniform.

Today, reservists and National Guard members are eligible for a newer version of the historic GI Bill through their service in the reserve components. Many reservists and guardsmen also qualify for educational assistance because of their earlier time on active duty.

MONTGOMERY GI BILL: SELECTED RESERVES

The major program during the 1990s that picks up the tab for military people and veterans to continue their education is the Montgomery GI Bill. Unlike earlier forms of the GI Bill, one version of the Montgomery GI Bill is specifically tailored for reservists and guard members.

Eligibility: There are several major thresholds that reservists and National Guard members must pass before they qualify for the Montgomery GI Bill. Recipients must meet all the following conditions:

- Be a member of the Selected Reserves, which includes people who attend drill periods with units and members of the Individual Mobilization Augmentation (IMA) manpower pool
- Enlisted: obligated to spend at least six years in Selected Reserves
- Officer: obligated to spend at least six years in Selected Reserves after initial obligation for military service
- Completed Initial Active Duty for Training (IADT)
- Met requirements for high school degree or equivalency certificate before completing IADT (In other words, the degree or certificate doesn't have to be in hand, but everything necessary to earn it must have been done.)
- Remain in good standing with unit or IMA officials

Most reservists and guard members lose eligibility for this educational benefit when they leave the Selected Reserves. This includes people who leave their reserve-component units or IMA slots for other reserve or guard duties and those who come on active duty.

People who lose eligibility because they leave the reserve components stop receiving Montgomery GI Bill benefits on the day of discharge.

For those staying in the reserve components, eligibility ends ten years after the date eligibility began, even if they're still in a qualifying drill unit or IMA position.

Those who lose eligibility because of the ten-year rule continue receiving GI Bill benefits through the end of the academic term. If enrolled in training without an academic term, eligibility can continue for twelve weeks beyond the tenth anniversary.

People who receive scholarships under the Reserve Officers' Training Corps (ROTC) program may not use the reserve version of the Montgomery GI Bill.

Eligibility continues for ten years after discharge for people who leave the Selected Reserves because of a medical disability or because of a formal drawdown program.

Many reserve-components members have already qualified for educational benefits under the more generous active-duty version of the Montgomery GI Bill. They retain eligibility for both versions of the Montgomery GI Bill, although they can't use both versions at the same time (see "Fine Points," below).

Contributions: Unlike the active-duty version of the Montgomery GI Bill, reservists and National Guard members don't have anything withheld from their paychecks for this benefit.

Payments: The maximum payment is $203 a month (1997 rate), and qualified reserve-component members can receive payments for thirty-six months.

The monthly rate usually increases every year by the same percentage as inflation. Everyone receiving payments under the reserve-component Montgomery GI Bill is eligible for those annual increases. No one is locked into a lower rate.

The maximum rate is for full-time schooling. Rates are also payable for one-quarter time, half-time, and three-quarter time. For example, reservists can receive seventy-two months of payments at the half-time rate.

Approved Courses: Participants must take classes or training that has been approved by the Department of Veterans Affairs.

In general, the following types of education and training are covered by the Montgomery GI Bill:

• College and university courses leading to undergraduate or graduate degrees

• Courses leading to diplomas or certificates from business, technical, or vocational schools

- Cooperative training, apprenticeships, and on-the-job training
- Correspondence courses and independent-study programs
- Tutorial assistance and remedial, refresher, or deficiency training
- Flight training

Just because a course fits into one of these categories doesn't mean that VA officials will automatically approve Montgomery GI Bill payments. Check with a benefits counselor at the nearest VA facility before assuming any financial obligations, especially when dealing with something other than a traditional, accredited college or university.

Fine Points: Some reservists are eligible to participate in both the active-duty and the reserve version of the Montgomery GI Bill, but there are limits.

Federal law prohibits them from being paid twice for the same class.

However, it may be possible for some people to use all their benefits under the active-duty program and then use their benefits under the reserve version, or vice versa. For them, there's a forty-eight-month total limit on benefits from all versions of the Montgomery GI Bill.

Other reservists may be eligible, simultaneously, for the reserve version of the Montgomery GI Bill and the Veterans Educational Assistance Program (VEAP).

MONTGOMERY GI BILL: ACTIVE DUTY

Reservists and National Guard members who qualified for the Montgomery GI Bill during earlier stints on active duty can use it even if they're eligible for the reserve-components version of the Montgomery GI Bill, although there are restrictions on using different versions at the same time.

Eligibility: Many reserve-component members earned rights to the active-duty Montgomery GI Bill during earlier periods of full-time service. They had $100 withheld for each of their first twelve months on active duty.

Reserve-component members can use GI Bill benefits earned on active duty.

Reserve-component members who come on active duty for extended periods may qualify for the active-duty version of the Montgomery GI Bill as long as:

• They hadn't refused to sign up for it during an earlier active-duty stint.

• They meet the normal time-on-active-duty requirements (two years for reduced benefits, three years for full benefits).

• They approve the customary withholding of $100 a month for twelve months.

Time Limit: Generally, the government stops writing checks for educational expenses that occur after the tenth anniversary of a veteran's discharge.

This ten-year "clock" can be reset if a veteran leaves active duty for at least ninety days and then returns.

Payments: The basic benefit under the Montgomery GI Bill varies by the amount of active-duty and reserve time. Here are the major categories, plus maximum payment rates in effect for 1997:

• $428 a month for thirty-six months to veterans with three years on active duty.

• $428 a month for thirty-six months to veterans with two years on active duty, followed by four years in Selected Reserves.

• $348 a month for thirty-six months to veterans with less than three years on active duty.

• Up to $700 a month in addition to one of the basic rates for people who enlisted or reenlisted in hard-to-fill jobs. This extra money is known as a "kicker."

Those who are eligible for "kickers" were officially notified when they enlisted or reenlisted.

No Refunds: Once a servicemember decides to participate in the Montgomery GI Bill, that decision cannot be changed, nor can the money be refunded.

Reserve-component members who qualify for both the active-duty and the reserve versions of the Montgomery GI Bill won't be repaid their $1,200 contributions to the active-duty program, even if they never use its benefits.

VETERANS EDUCATIONAL ASSISTANCE PROGRAM (VEAP)

Between the end of the Vietnam-era GI Bill and the creation of the Montgomery GI Bill, a program called the Veterans Educational Assistance Program (VEAP) was enacted. Some people can still use its benefits.

Eligibility: Participants first became members of the military between January 1, 1977, and July 1, 1985. To receive benefits today, participants must have had some money withheld from their military paychecks before April 1, 1987.

Contributions and Payments: VEAP is a dollar-for-dollar matching program. For every dollar contributed by a servicemember, the government adds two dollars to be used to pay educational bills.

> VEAP-eligible veterans can reapply after they've "cashed out" their benefits.

The maximum contribution by a servicemember toward VEAP is $2,700. After the government adds its share, the most the majority of veterans receive from VEAP is $8,100.

Some Army veterans, however, receive more, known as "kickers," for taking hard-to-fill jobs.

Payments for education under VEAP end ten years after a veteran's discharge.

With the GI Bill: It's possible for veterans to get financial help under both VEAP and the reserve-version of the Montgomery GI Bill, but both programs cannot be used to pay for the same course.

Check with a military education counselor or a VA benefits counselor before trying to use VEAP and any version of the GI Bill at the same time.

19

HOME LOANS

In This Chapter:

- *Eligibility*
- *Qualifying Homes*
- *Home Loan Details*

Since the end of World War II, one of the military's major tools to persuade young Americans to spend a few years in uniform has been the prospect of earning a so-called GI Bill home loan.

This is a benefit that hasn't eroded over the decades. In fact, it's been expanded to include members of the reserves and National Guard and veterans whose military service consisted solely of time in the reserve components.

ELIGIBILITY

Members of the reserves and National Guard must meet three basic eligibility requirements to qualify for GI Bill home loans.

First, recipients must be members of the Selected Reserves, which includes most people assigned to reserve units, National Guard units, the trained manpower pool known at the Individual Mobilization Augmentation (IMA) program, full-time unit support personnel, and some trainees.

Second, reservists and National Guard members must have spent six years in the Selected Reserves before seeking to use this benefit.

Third, the reserve-component member must fall into one of the following categories:

- Still in Selected Reserves
- Discharged under honorable conditions
- Retired
- Transferred to Ready Reserves

Many new reservists and National Guard members qualify for the GI Bill home loan program before their first drill period because of active-duty service.

To qualify for a GI Bill home loan through active-duty service, people must usually spend at least 180 continuous days on active duty. That time limit dropped to 90 days during the Persian Gulf War.

The widowed spouses of two kinds of reserve-component members can qualify for GI Bill home loans. The military spouse must have died while on active duty—regardless of the duration of active duty—or died after leaving the military from a service-connected medical condition.

Once a servicemember is eligible, GI Bill home loans are a lifetime benefit. GI Bill home loans can be used to buy more than one home.

> Financial institutions have a voice in deciding whether a veteran is a reasonable credit risk.

A final eligibility point shouldn't be overlooked. The money that's actually loaned for a GI Bill home loan comes from a bank, a mortgage company, or another financial institution. Those companies decide whether someone is financially capable of paying the mortgage each month.

Veterans who believe that they've been unfairly turned

down for a home loan because of race, gender, or their veteran's status should notify the nearest office of the Department of Veterans Affairs.

QUALIFYING HOMES

Not every type of home or every type of transaction can qualify for a government-backed VA home loan. Here are the major uses:

- To buy a home
- To buy a town house or condominium
- To buy a manufactured or mobile home
- To buy a lot for a manufactured home
- To build a home
- To repair, alter, or improve a home
- To make energy-efficient improvements
- To purchase and, simultaneously, to improve a home
- To purchase a manufactured home and improve the lot
- To refinance an existing home loan
- To refinance an existing home loan to reduce the interest rate
- To refinance a manufactured home loan and acquire a lot

> Widows and widowers of some veterans qualify for GI Bill home loans.

VA home-loan guarantees can be used to purchase or to build residential property containing more than one family unit. However, there cannot be more than four family units, and the veteran must occupy one of them.

Before any loans are approved, a VA appraiser must establish the market value of the home. The goal is to ensure that, since the government must repay the loan if the veteran defaults, the home itself is a reasonable financial risk for the government.

HOME LOAN DETAILS

Although this VA program is commonly called a home loan (a phrase that is even used here), remember that it's actually a guarantee. The government promises that it will pay the company issuing the mortgage if the veteran defaults on the loan.

Application: Reserve-component members seeking a VA home loan should apply at the nearest office of the Department of Veterans Affairs for a document called a *Certificate of Eligibility.* They'll have to prove that they have enough qualifying time in the reserves or guard.

Veterans should provide VA officials with a copy of their formal discharge papers, now called a DD Form 214.

Interest Rates: VA home loan guarantees must be obtained for fixed-rate loans. The government doesn't set the interest rate. That's between the veteran and the lender.

Down Payments: VA rules may require a down payment to purchase a manufactured or mobile home, for lots, and for homes whose price exceeds the property's fair-market value.

Most lenders don't require down payments for GI Bill home loans, but that's their decision. They can ask a veteran for a down payment.

Funding Fee: To offset the government's losses when veterans default on their loans, a funding fee is applied to all GI Bill home loans. It's a certain percentage of the total home loan.

Here are the 1997 funding fees for specific categories:

Loans with no down payment or down payments less than 5 percent: 2.75 percent for reserve veterans, 2 percent for active-duty veterans.

Loans for refinancing, home improvement, home repair: 2.75 percent for reserve veterans, 2 percent for active-duty veterans.

For second or subsequent use, with a downpayment of less than 5 percent: 3 percent; with a down payment of at least

5 percent: 1.5 percent; with a down payment of at least 10 percent: 1.25 percent.

Loans for purchase or new construction with a down payment of at least 5 percent but less than 10 percent: 2.5 percent for reserve veterans, 1.5 percent for active-duty veterans.

Loans for purchase or construction with a down payment of at least 10 percent: 2 percent for reserve veterans, 1.25 percent for active-duty veteran.

Manufactured or mobile homes: 1 percent for both reserve and active-duty veterans.

Interest-rate reduction loans: 0.5 percent for both reserve and active-duty veterans.

Assumption of another veteran's VA home loan: 0.5 percent for both reserve and active-duty veterans.

Closing Costs: Incidental expenses, called closing costs, are paid by everyone buying, building, or refinancing a home. They can be charged to people receiving GI Bill home loans.

Discount "Points": Reserve-component members and veterans can be asked to pay "points" to GI Bill home loan purchases.

Prepayments: The lender cannot penalize any GI Bill participant who pays off the mortgage ahead of schedule.

Selling: Reserve-component members and veterans can buy more than one home with the GI Bill, but they can buy only one at a time. They can't let someone else assume the original mortgage.

Financial Problems: If a temporary setback such as a job loss or unusual expenses results in a veteran's being unable to pay the regular monthly mortgage, there is some limited protection for people with VA-backed loans.

20

LIFE INSURANCE

In This Chapter:

- *Reserve, Guard, and Active Duty*
- *Veterans*
- *Disabled Veterans*

Members of the reserve components have the same financial responsibilities toward their families as their civilian counterparts. And, because they occasionally must put on uniforms and march into harm's way, they may face greater risks than the typical wage earner.

The government recognizes that it has a responsibility to help reservists and National Guard members help themselves. Several government-backed insurance programs are on the books for part-time military members, offering better benefits at lower costs than those available in the private sector.

RESERVE, GUARD, AND ACTIVE DUTY

The major government-backed insurance program for reservists and National Guard members is Servicemember's Group Life Insurance (SGLI), the same plan offered to the active-duty force, with special adaptations for the reserve components.

Eligibility: Some reserve-component members are eligible for full-time SGLI coverage. Others are eligible for part-time SGLI coverage that takes effect only when they're in uniform.

Most reserve-component members who are ineligible for SGLI coverage qualify for government-backed Veterans Group Life Insurance (VGLI) coverage, discussed later in this chapter.

Full-time coverage: To qualify for full-time SGLI coverage, reservists and guardsmen must meet two criteria:

• They must be assigned to a unit or to an individual personnel "slot" that requires them to perform at least twelve drill periods (or, more formally, inactive-duty training periods) a year. Those drill periods must meet the military's standards for receiving credit for retirement purposes.

• They must be members of what's formally known as the Ready Reserve. This includes drilling members of reserve-component units, reservists, and National Guard members in full-time support positions, plus members of the Individual Mobilization Augmentation (IMA) program. It also can include members of the Individual Ready Reserve (IRR) and Inactive National Guard (ING).

Note that IRR and ING members must also satisfy the first requirement—being in a position that requires twelve drill periods a year—for SGLI coverage. Here, the word "require" is important. Military members must be in a position that officially obliges them to attend twelve drill periods.

Full-time coverage also extends to other categories of reserve-component members:

• Reserve-component members during the first 120 days after losing full-time SGLI coverage

• Reservists and guard members during the first year after they leave the Ready Reserve with a disability that's officially rated as total

For many years, retired reserve-component members also qualified for full-time SGLI coverage. That ended in January 1997.

Part-time coverage: Many reservists and National Guard members who don't meet the rules for full-time SGLI benefits are covered during specific periods, usually lasting only a few days.

This part-time SGLI coverage applies to people who have orders specifying that, for a period of less than thirty-one days, they will be on active duty or active duty for training. They have SGLI coverage during those days of service, plus during travel to and from the training site.

This part-time coverage goes to those who aren't members of the Ready Reserve but who are scheduled to attend drill periods. They have SGLI coverage from the moment they leave home until the moment they return home.

Dual Eligibility: People with VGLI coverage may find themselves in a position also to qualify for SGLI coverage. A servicemember can be covered by both at the same time, but the total coverage in 1997 was capped at $200,000.

Rates and Rules: The minimum amount of SGLI coverage available is $10,000; the maximum is $200,000. Between these two figures, people can obtain coverage in multiples of $10,000.

A single SGLI rate applies to everyone. In 1997, the rate was 85 cents a month for each $10,000 of coverage. Thus the full $200,000 in coverage cost $17 a month.

Reserve-component members who are eligible for 120 days of SGLI after their full-time Ready Reserve policies end don't have to pay premiums for the coverage.

Also not required to pay SGLI premiums are reservists and National Guard members with total disabilities related to their military service. They receive free SGLI coverage for a year.

Beneficiaries: An SGLI beneficiary can be any person; it doesn't have to be a relative. It can also be a firm, a corporation, the veteran's own estate, or any legal entity.

To avoid legal complications, however, that decision should be submitted to the SGLI administrator on the official beneficiary designation form, which can be obtained from military personnel offices or VA regional offices.

SGLI participants can change their beneficiaries at any time.

Application: Everyone eligible for SGLI is automatically enrolled in the program for $100,000 of coverage. To obtain more coverage, less coverage, or no coverage, the servicemember must request it.

After Discharge: Active-duty members with SGLI and most reserve SGLI participants are covered by their insurance policies—at no cost—for 120 days after discharge.

VETERANS

Most people who leave the military—either active duty or the reserve components—can purchase life insurance at low group rates under a program called Veterans Group Life Insurance (VGLI).

Eligibility: To qualify for VGLI, a military member must:

- Be released from military service after August 1, 1974,
- Be a member of the Individual Ready Reserve (IRR) or Inactive National Guard (ING), or
- Be a disabled reservist with a disability incurred while on inactive duty for training or while on active duty for less than thirty-one days.

> Some reservists and guard members qualify for VGLI and SGLI at the same time. They have a total $200,000 limit on coverage.

What are the eligibility rules for military retirees? For recipients of exit bonuses? For veterans with early releases or continued obligations to spend time in the reserves? The answer to all these questions—and more—lies in the first broad eligibility rule. As long as they left active duty after August 1, 1974, these people are eligible.

This broad eligibility window includes retired reserve-component members and so-called gray-area retirees.

Dual Eligibility: People with VGLI coverage may also qualify for SGLI coverage. They can be covered by both at the same time, but the total coverage in 1997 was capped at $200,000.

Rates and Rules: Coverage can be for as little as $10,000, as much as $200,000, or any amount in between, in $10,000 increments.

Every qualifying veteran can get at least $100,000 in coverage. But between $100,000 and $200,000, the amount of VGLI can't be greater than the amount of SGLI coverage they had while on active duty.

To receive this benefit, reserve-component members must pay a monthly premium, which is based on age. Here are the monthly premiums for each $10,000 in coverage (1997 rates):

- Age 29 or younger: $1.20
- Age 30–34: $2.00
- Age 35–39: $2.60
- Age 40–44: $3.40
- Age 45–49: $4.40
- Age 50–54: $6.50
- Age 55–59: $8.80
- Age 60–64: $11.25
- Age 65–69: $15.00
- Age 70–74: $22.50
- Age 75 and older: $45.00

Since 1993, veterans have been eligible to purchase VGLI coverage for life.

Beneficiaries: A VGLI beneficiary can be any person; it doesn't have to be a relative. It can also be a firm, a corporation, the veteran's own estate, or any legal entity.

To avoid legal complications, that decision should be submitted to the VGLI administrator on the official beneficiary designation form. The administrator is the office to which the premium checks are mailed.

VGLI participants can change their beneficiaries at any time.

Application: Veterans must apply for VGLI coverage within a year of being discharged. By applying earlier—within 120 days of discharge—they get a break by not having to undergo a physical examination.

DISABLED VETERANS

The government's involvement with military members doesn't end when they take off the uniform. Two programs are on the books to help veterans with service-connected disabilities.

Former members of the reserve components can qualify for these programs, as long as they meet the normal eligibility rules.

Service-Disabled Veterans Insurance (SDVI): This is life insurance for people with service-connected disabilities that make them ineligible for private-sector insurance.

SDVI is free for veterans who are officially rated as 100 percent disabled. Veterans with lesser disabilities must pay premiums, although government subsidies keep the rates low.

Total coverage is capped at $10,000 (1997 rate).

Veterans Mortgage Life Insurance (VMLI): This is mortgage insurance for veterans with extreme disabilities. They must have disabilities that are officially considered service connected, and they must be participating in the VA's specially adapted housing program, which modifies homes for people with severe disabilities.

Participants pay a premium, usually by having the government withhold money from their monthly VA disability compensation checks. The exact amount of the premium is based on complex formulas.

21

REEMPLOYMENT RIGHTS

In This Chapter:

- *Eligibility*
- *Employee Rights*
- *Leaving Work*
- *Returning to Work*
- *Five-Year Limit*
- *Vacation Time*
- *Problems*

The government has an important interest in ensuring that the civilian careers of its citizen-soldiers aren't jeopardized by part-time military service. Reserve-component members have rights written into federal law, especially the Uniformed Services Employment and Reemployment Rights Act (USERRA) of 1994.

Although most of *Reservist's Money Guide* deals with dollars-and-cents programs that put money into military paychecks, this chapter focuses on the laws that ensure that reservists and National Guard members have civilian paychecks once they leave military service.

ELIGIBILITY

Two sets of factors affect eligibility for reemployment rights in private-sector jobs. One set involves the military, the other the civilian job.

Military Factors: Reemployment rights for private-sector jobs extend to most people in uniform—active duty, reserve-component members on extended active duty, reserve-component members on shorter stints of active duty, and reserve-component members on inactive duty or drill periods.

There's no differentiation between involuntary call-ups and people who volunteer for active duty, including active duty for training.

Reservists and guard members must be released from active duty under honorable conditions. Employers don't have to reemploy people who develop problems on active duty that result in an adverse discharge.

Job Factors: All employers—private sector, federal government, local and state governments—are required by federal law to reemploy certain workers who seek their jobs after leaving military service, with the following conditions:

- The job that the person left to go on active duty must be a permanent job.
- The employee must go directly from the job to the military.
- The employee must give reasonable notice to the employer of the call-up. (Rule of thumb: Employees should tell their employers as soon as they find out.)
- The employee must report to the job within a reasonable time after leaving military service (discussed in more detail later).
- The employee cannot spend more than five years, total, on active duty (also discussed later).

Employers cannot deny reemployment rights to military personnel because the job they left has been eliminated in their absence.

EMPLOYEE RIGHTS

Eligible military members returning to civilian employers aren't necessarily guaranteed their old jobs. They can be comparable jobs, in terms of pay, status, and seniority. But they must also be comparable to what the employees would have gotten if they'd never gone on full-time military service.

For people on active duty for ninety-one days or more, that can mean that if they would have been promoted if they'd stayed on the job, they must be given that promotion after returning from the military. "Promotion" can be defined in terms of pay, position, or seniority.

If a person's civilian skills have been hurt by an absence from the job market, the civilian employer must make a reasonable effort to retrain or requalify the employee. If a former military member can't be retrained, the employer can offer a lesser-skilled job, although the employee retains seniority.

Employers must make reasonable efforts to place employees with service-connected health problems in civilian jobs.

Health care is another employee right. People who leave their civilian jobs for military duty can choose to retain employer-sponsored health insurance.

> Reemployment rights affect more than pay. They also involve seniority, health care, vacation time, and promotions.

If the military service is thirty days or less, employers can require ex-employees to pay normal health insurance premiums. For coverage starting on the thirty-first day, employers can require reserve-component members to pay their usual health insurance premiums, plus the employer's per-employee cost, plus another 2 percent. Put another way, people may have to pay 102 percent of the total per-employee cost of health care.

For those who decide to keep employer-sponsored health insurance, eligibility ends on the day after the deadline for reapplying for their old jobs (discussed later).

Regardless whether people retain employer-provided health insurance while on active duty, they are entitled to immediate coverage by their employer's health insurance plan after returning to work. Immediate coverage also goes to family members previously covered.

Some employers grant benefits such as holiday pay or employer-subsidized life insurance to nonmilitary employees on furloughs or leaves of absence. If nonmilitary employees get these benefits, the same benefits must go to former employees on full-time military service.

People accrue seniority in their civilian jobs during their military services when it comes to issues such as rates of pay, pension vesting, and credit for time for pensions.

LEAVING WORK

Employers have the right to advance warning when one of their employees is leaving the job for military training or active duty.

How much warning is enough? The law doesn't say.

But if the employer is given the same notification as the military gives the reservist, no fault can be found.

RETURNING TO WORK

Federal law has specific timetables for when reserve-component members should return to their civilian jobs if they intend to claim reemployment rights. Those limits are based on the duration of the active-duty stint:

- For active-duty periods of thirty consecutive days or less, the reservist and guardsman must go directly from the active-duty site to home by the safest manner. After arriving home, they are allowed eight hours' rest and are expected to be on the job for the first work period beginning after that eight-hour period.
- For periods of 31 to 180 days, the employee must request reemployment within 14 days after completing military service.
- For periods of 181 days or more, the employee must request reemployment within 90 days after completing service.

All periods can be extended for two years when people are hospitalized for or are convalescing from service-connected injuries or illnesses.

FIVE-YEAR LIMIT

Reservists and National Guard members retain reemployment rights with civilian employers as long as they don't spend more than five years away from their jobs on military service.

That's five years total, not five consecutive years.

Some kinds of military service—actually, the most common kinds of active duty—aren't counted against that five-year total. Not counted toward the five-year limit are the following:

- Service during wartime, national emergencies, and contingency operations
- Drills, annual training, and other training judged by the military to be for professional development and skill training
- For reservists and guardsmen, active duty for initial training that requires more than five years (usually for aviators)
- For National Guard members, state call-ups

The five years applies to time away from a single employer. As far as the government is concerned, a reservist or guardsman can take twenty years away from a civilian job, so long as it's with four different employers.

Different time limits and different ways of reckoning time were in effect before the current USERRA was passed in 1994. Still, time away from a civilian job before USERRA's enactment on December 12, 1994, is counted toward the five-year limit.

VACATION TIME

Going on active duty for training or for a major operation isn't a vacation. Federal law prohibits employers from depriving workers of vacation time because they've been away from the job on military service.

Private-sector employees can't be forced to take their annual vacation time when they're on active duty.

Federal employees are entitled to fifteen days of paid military leave per year. After exhausting those fifteen days, they can choose to use accrued annual leave or to take unpaid leave.

PROBLEMS

Discriminating against reserve-component members in the workplace is illegal, and the federal government can take employers who discriminate to court. This includes employers who refuse to rehire mobilized guardsmen and reservists; deny them promotions, training, or other opportunities for advancement; or make other reprisals.

> Commanders should be involved early in any dispute affecting a reservist's reemployment rights.

The language of federal law contains a key legal distinction. Reserve-component members don't have to prove that an adverse action was linked to reserve service. Rather, the employer has to prove that it would have taken the adverse action even if the employee hadn't been in the reserves or guard.

The first step for any reserve-component member with a problem is that person's commander. Many problems arise because employers have bad information about the rights of reservists and guard members.

Another option is to contact a local representative of the Veterans Employment and Training Service (VETS). Local VETS offices are listed in the blue pages of the phone book under "U.S. Government—Department of Labor."

A final option is to contact the National Committee for Employer Support of the Guard and Reserves. It's in Washington, D.C., and the telephone number in 1997 was 1-800-336-4590.

This national committee has trained ombudsmen who help individual reservists and guardsmen. However, those counselors will expect callers to have worked already with their commanders or local VETS officials.

PART V

SPECIAL TIMES, SPECIAL CASES

22

DISCHARGE PAYS

In This Chapter:

- *Final Pay*
- *Separation Pay*
- *Preretirement Separation*
- *Disability Severance Pay*

When members of the military approach the end of their time in uniform, they're eligible for a wide array of benefits, programs, and payments to ease their return to the private sector.

The focus here is on programs that put—or directly translate into—money in the pockets of folks leaving the armed forces. Also discussed are some other benefits that have a financial impact on soon-to-be veterans.

FINAL BENEFITS

Military people are entitled to the full range of pay, allowances, and benefits until the last minute of the last day that they're in uniform.

Eligibility: Reserve-component members on active duty—regardless of the kind of active-duty service or its duration—are entitled to one-thirtieth the usual monthly rate of Basic Pay, the Basic Allowance for Quarters (BAQ), and the officer's

Basic Allowance for Subsistence (BAS) for each day on active duty. (Enlisted BAS is normally calculated as a daily rate.)

Other elements of the military paycheck have their own rules, which are discussed in the appropriate chapters. Some result in a daily rate, others in payment of the full monthly rate if someone qualifies for single day.

Reservists and National Guard members discharged directly from inactive-duty status are eligible for any Drill Pay that they've earned, plus any special kinds of pay. Again, see the appropriate chapters of this book for the payment schedules for these bonuses.

Taxes are usually deducted from the final military paycheck, as are any sums owed the government.

Cashed-in Leave: People earn leave while on active duty, and if they are discharged before using those leave days, they can cash in any unused leave.

One day of cashed-in leave is equal to one-thirtieth of the Basic Pay appropriate for a person's rank and years of service. No other element of the military paycheck is used to calculate the value of unused leave.

Reserve-component members on extended active duty are credited with thirty days of leave annually.

Reservists on full-time service for at least thirty-one days earn two and a half days of leave for each month on active duty. The services have their own rules for deciding when reserve-component members on active duty switch from earning two and a half days per month to thirty days per year.

Normally, reservists and guard members receive one retirement "point" for each day on leave, but cashed-in leave cannot be converted into retirement points.

Government-Paid Transportation: People discharged from full-time military duty qualify for government-paid shipment of household goods, plus financial help moving their families and themselves.

Reservists and National Guard members on shorter active-duty stints qualify for government benefits to transport themselves and a limited amount of personal property. Usually, this applies to reserve-component members on active duty for less than twenty weeks in one location, which includes annual two-week summer camps.

Members of the reserve components who are discharged from inactive-duty status aren't eligible for any government benefits to move themselves, their families, or their household goods to a new location.

Health Insurance: Reservists and guardsmen leaving full-time military service can purchase special government-backed health insurance for themselves and their family members.

Ineligible are reserve-component members on short stints of active duty, plus reservists and guard members being discharged while on inactive-duty status.

Called the Continued Health Care Benefit Program, this plan offers medical coverage for a maximum of eighteen months. Coverage for shorter periods is possible, but coverage comes in three-month blocks.

This benefit isn't automatic. Those who want it must apply for it before discharge (transition, personnel, or finance offices should have applications).

Also, it isn't free. In 1997, the premiums for a three-month period were about $933 for individuals and about $1,196 for families.

Recipients of Separation Pay, the Voluntary Separation Incentive (VSI), and the Special Separation Benefit (SSB) are eligible for medical care in on-base facilities under CHAMPUS and Tricare for up to 120 days after discharge. Some exit-bonus recipients have a shorter post-discharge period of coverage.

People whose health was damaged by injury or illness while on active or inactive duty may be eligible for lifetime medical care as recipients of VA Disability Compensation.

Unemployment Compensation: Most people leaving full-time active duty are eligible for unemployment compensation, which is a government-run program that provides a minimum income to workers who are between jobs.

Usually ineligible are reserve-component members coming off two-week stints of active duty, and other short periods on active duty and inactive-duty status.

Twenty-six weeks is the longest that anyone can receive unemployment compensation. Rates vary from state to state. In 1997, the average weekly payment was slightly more than $200.

Military retirees are usually ineligible for unemployment compensation. People with dishonorable discharges may or may not be eligible, depending on the reason for the discharge. States impose a variety of restrictions on recipients of exit bonuses.

Applications for unemployment compensation are usually made through state employment offices, which are listed under "State Government" in the telephone book. Veterans should bring several copies of their discharge papers, DD Form 214, when applying.

SEPARATION PAY

Separation Pay is given to mid-career military people with good records who've been involuntarily selected for discharge, usually to meet manpower goals within their specialties.

It is sometimes called Nondisability Separation Pay to distinguish it from Disability Severance Pay, which is also discussed in this chapter. It's also referred to as Involuntary Separation Pay.

This chapter deals with Separation Pay offered to members of the reserve component who are not on active duty. A different program—with the same name—exists for active-duty people who are forced from full-time military service.

Eligibility: Separation Pay can be given to officers and enlisted members who meet some basic qualifications:

• They must be members of the Selected Reserves, which includes people assigned to reserve-component units and those in the Individual Manpower Augmentation (IMA) pool.

• They must have at least six years of military service—active-duty years, plus "good" years as reservists or guardsmen—but less than fifteen years.

• They must have been selected by their parent service for involuntary discharge from the reserve components, through no fault of their own.

Rates: Separation Pay is a one-time lump-sum bonus. It is fully taxable.

> Separation pay isn't a right. The military decides who will be offered it.

Rank, years on active duty, and reserve-component "points" all come into play in the formula used to determine an individual's Separation Pay. The formula is long, but it's fairly easy:

1. Add together the points earned in the reserve components.
2. Count the number of days on active duty.
3. Add the points from Step 1 to the days from Step 2.
4. Divide the number reached in Step 3 by 365. Set that figure aside for a moment.
5. Figure out the monthly Basic Pay that would be received on active duty.
6. Convert the monthly Basic Pay figure into a daily figure by dividing by 30.
7. Multiply the daily Basic Pay determined in Step 6 by 62.
8. Multiply the dollar amount reached in Step 7 by the figure determined in Step 4.
9. Finally, multiply the dollar amount reached in Step 8 by 15 percent.

What's left is the amount of Separation Pay, which ranges from $600 to $6,000.

Other Rules: Separation Pay recipients who later qualify for other payments from the military have 75 percent of that additional military income withheld until they've repaid the government for their Separation Pay. Types of pay that are withheld include:

- Basic Pay
- Drill Pay
- Retired pay
- VA Disability Compensation

Recipients of Separation Pay are not military retirees. Their connection to the government ends on the day of their discharge from the reserves or guard. But like all veterans, they can seek benefits offered by the Department of Veterans Affairs.

The reserve components don't have a version of two widely discussed active-duty exit bonuses, the Voluntary Separation Incentive (VSI) and the Special Separation Benefit (SSB).

PRERETIREMENT SEPARATION

Not everyone who qualifies for military retired pay takes off his uniform. The military has at least one financial tool to persuade reserve-component members who could retire to leave their units or the personnel slots they fill during mobilizations.

Eligibility: Recipients of preretirement separation benefits must have twenty "good" or "creditable" years, according to the military's method for calculating reserve-component time. In addition, they must not have reached their sixtieth birthdays, which is when reservists and National Guard members begin receiving retired pay.

They must also be members of the Selected Reserves, which includes people assigned to reserve-component units and people in the manpower pool known as the Individual Mobilization Augmentation (IMA) program.

Manpower planners decide who will be offered this bonus. Reservists and guard members who refuse it may be transferred involuntarily from their units or IMA slots.

Rates: Recipients get an annual lump-sum payment from the military. The amounts are based on Basic Pay and a person's number of "good" years.

The formula for computing rates begins with the Basic Pay appropriate for an individual's rank and number of years in service.

The monthly rate for Basic Pay is multiplied by 12 to yield the yearly rate for Basic Pay.

Then comes a "multiplier." For everyone, the minimum is 5 percent. For each year of service beyond twenty years, add 1/2 percent. For example, the multiplier for those with twenty-one years is 5 1/2 percent; for twenty-two years, it's 6 percent; for twenty-three years, it's 6 1/2 percent; and so on (fractions of years don't count).

Multiply the multiplier by the yearly Basic Pay rate. What's left is the annual payment.

The maximum multiplier is 10 percent. To get that, a person needs to have thirty years of service and still be under sixty years of age.

Five years is the longest that reserve-component members can receive this bonus, and one year is the minimum. This means that no one can receive this bonus for the first time if it is within twelve months of his sixtieth birthday.

This payment is taxable. It doesn't decrease or delay the amount of retired pay that qualified reserve-component members receive.

Until they reach their sixtieth birthday and begin receiving retired pay, recipients of this bonus are still classified by the military as not receiving retired pay.

DISABILITY SEVERANCE PAY

Several programs are available for people unable to fulfill their military duties because of service-related medical problems. Disability Severance Pay—also known as Medical Severance Pay—goes to people with relatively mild problems. (Chapter 24 has details about benefits for those with more severe health problems.)

Eligibility: Reserve-component members on all kinds of active duty, plus those on inactive-duty status, can qualify for Disability Severance Pay.

Eligibility also extends to reservists and National Guard members traveling to training sites and back home again and to those traveling for weekend drill periods, annual active duty training, and other active-duty activities.

Four major groups are *ineligible* for Disability Severance Pay:

• Those with less than six months in the military (including reserve time calculated at the rate of one day per "point")

• People with disabilities caused while incarcerated, while absent without leave, or through willful misconduct

• Those with at least twenty years on active duty (they're eligible for regular length-of-service retirement, discussed in Chapter 24)

• Servicemembers with disabilities officially rated as being at least 30 percent (they can qualify for a more generous military disability retirement, discussed in Chapter 24)

> VA Disability Compensation is the financial backbone of government efforts to help disabled veterans.

One of the military's Physical Evaluation Boards must select a reservist or National Guard member for discharge under conditions that allow payment of Disability Severance Pay.

Rates: Disability Severance Pay is a one-time lump-sum payment given to qualified servicemembers, usually on their last day in the military.

A simple two-step formula—with some unexpected fine print—is used to calculate amounts:

- Multiply the monthly Basic Pay by two.
- Take that figure and multiply it by the number of years in the military.

Reservists and National Guard members must convert "points" to months. That is, for every thirty points, they're credited with one month under this formula.

Years aren't counted as fractions. Periods of six months or more are rounded up to the higher year. Periods less than six months are rounded down to the lower year.

Some people have held higher ranks than the ones they have during their last days in uniform. The military lets them use the Basic Pay of that higher rank in this formula. This applies to people who:

- Hold a higher reserve rank
- Served satisfactorily in a higher rank, even a temporary one
- Had a disability discovered during a prepromotion medical examination

In this last instance, military members whose disabilities were discovered during prepromotion physicals are eligible to use the rank they would have held if they'd been promoted.

Taxes: The general rule on Disability Severance Pay is that it's taxable. Certain narrowly defined groups of people can receive tax-free payments, but they are the exception.

Eligible for tax-free payments are people whose Disability Severance Pay is based on health problems caused by:

- Armed conflict
- Hazardous service
- "Conditions simulating war"
- "An instrumentality of war," such as terrorism

Other Rules: Recipients of Disability Severance Pay who later qualify for VA Disability Compensation lose one dollar of VA money for every dollar of Disability Severance Pay received.

People who receive Disability Severance Pay aren't considered military retirees. Their connection with the military is ended when they leave active duty. They are ineligible for care in military hospitals or for other on-base services.

23

Retired and Disability Pays

In This Chapter:

- *Typical Retired Pay*
- *Fifteen-Year Retired Pay*
- *Incapacitation Pay*
- *Temporary Disability Retirement*
- *Military Disability Retirement*
- *VA Disability Compensation*

People who devote a significant portion of their lives to the military—even reserve-component members who measure that commitment one weekend at a time—are entitled to special treatment by the government. That includes a monthly pension, certain medical benefits, and access to on-base resources such as commissaries and exchanges.

Also entitled to lifelong financial help from the government are the men and women whose health has been permanently harmed by their military service. For them, the Department of Veterans Affairs may be called on to supplement the military's programs.

TYPICAL RETIRED PAY

Although the reserve retirement system has some broad similarities with the active-duty retirement system, it's not as generous. Twenty years in the reserves won't yield the same retired pay as twenty years on active duty.

Eligibility: Reservists and National Guard members must accumulate twenty years that are officially rated as "good" or "creditable." A good or creditable year is one in which a reservist accumulates at least fifty "points."

Reserve Retired Pay Summary

Purpose:	Pension, deferred pay for lower active-duty pay
Amount:	Date of entry into the military defines the system
Rate:	By a formula that includes rank, years of service, and "points"
Taxable:	Yes
Garnishable:	Yes
Problem areas:	No payment until age sixty; accumulating "good" years; must spend last eight years in reserves

Reservists and guardsmen receive one point for each day on active duty, whether during a period of years on active duty or during a typical two-week summer camp. They also receive one point for each drill period (meaning that they get four points for a typical weekend drill), and for certain blocks of instruction.

Usually, the fifty points must be accumulated during the 365-day period that starts with the anniversary of their entry into the reserves.

There's also a time-in-the-reserves rule. Normally, reservists and guard members must spend their last eight years in uniform as members of a reserve component. That figure was reduced, temporarily, to six years during the post–Cold War drawdown, but it's scheduled to return to eight years in 1999.

What if a person spent eighteen years on active duty? Can't that person qualify for reserve-component retirement in another two years? No. That eighteen-year active-duty veteran would normally have to spend another eight years as a reservist or National Guard member. In that case, retired pay would be based on twenty-six years of active-duty and reserve-component service.

Reserve-component members don't begin receiving retired pay until their sixtieth birthday. Typically, that leaves a gap of many years between the time reservists and guard members become eligible for retired pay and the time they actually receive it.

Two Retirement Systems: Two different military retirement systems are available to reservists and guardsmen. Reserve-component members are covered by the retirement plan in effect when they first joined the military.

Each plan has a way of defining "years" that's different from the ordinary meaning of the word and even from the military's method discussed in the "Eligibility" section above.

For the retirement formulas, a year is equal to 360 "points" earned by active duty, inactive duty, and comparable training.

The two plans are:

Basic Plan: Covers people who first joined the military on September 7, 1980, or on an earlier date. They are eligible for 2.5 percent of the last monthly amount of Basic Pay for each year of service. This plan uses the Basic Pay rate appropriate for the servicemember's rank and years of service that's in effect on the veteran's sixtieth birthday.

High-Three Plan: Covers people who joined the military

after September 7, 1980. The retirement formula is based on average monthly Basic Pay for the highest three years—or, more properly, thirty-six months—of service. These people are eligible for 2.5 percent of the "high-three" average for each year of service. This plan uses the Basic Pay rates that were actually in effect for the thirty-six months before receiving retired pay.

Both retirement systems limit retired pay to 75 percent of Basic Pay. Both also provide full cost-of-living adjustments (COLAs), usually every year, to protect the purchasing power of retired pay from inflation.

People qualifying for active-duty retirement have three retirement systems. A third active-duty plan, which doesn't cover reserve retirees, applies to people who first joined the military after July 31, 1986. It's called the Redux Plan. Reserve-component retirement for people who join the military after July 1986 is based on the High-Three Plan.

Rates: Determining the retired pay of a specific reservist or National Guard member is a five-step process.

1. Add up the number of points earned throughout the reservist's military career, both active duty and in the reserves.
2. Divide those points by 360 to convert points into years.
3. Multiply the number reached in Step 2 by 2.5 percent. Set that figure aside for a moment.
4. Find the monthly Basic Pay appropriate for the retiree's rank and years of service. (For retirees under the High-Three Plan, add together the monthly Basic Pay in effect for the last thirty-six months of peak military earning, then divide by thirty-six to get a monthly average.)
5. Multiply the dollar amount reached in Step 4 by the percentage figure developed in Step 3. What's left is the initial monthly check for retired pay.

When converting points to years, carry the calculation to three figures to the right of the decimal point, then round to two figures to the right of the decimal point. Take, as an example, someone with 4,736 points. Dividing that total by 360 yields 13.155 years. That would be rounded to 13.16 years.

Divorce: Federal law permits state divorce judges to award a portion of a military retiree's pension to an ex-spouse as part of a divorce settlement. Once these settlements have been approved by a judge, a military finance center can send that money directly to the ex-spouse (for more information, see Chapter 25).

Federal Employment: With one exception, if retired reservists or retired guard members work as federal civil servants, there is no effect on either their military retired pay or their civil service salaries.

The exception involves people whose combined retired pay and civil service salary exceed $108,200 in 1997. This limit usually rises each year by the same rate as salary increases for federally employed civilians.

People whose income exceeds this limit lose however much retired pay is necessary to stay under the limit. The most they can lose is 100 percent of retired pay. A military retiree whose civil service salary alone exceeds the level is allowed to keep the total civilian salary.

Military retired pay and federal civil service salaries are the only two sources of income included in this withholding. Retirees subjected to this formula have their full pensions restored when they leave these top-paying civil service jobs.

Reserve-component retirees are unaffected by a similar so-called dual-compensation restriction that affects only officers with regular commissions. Retired regular officers who are federally employed civilians can keep about the first $10,000 in annual retired pay, plus half the remaining retired pay.

Taxes: The normal twenty-year military retirement pay is fully taxable for federal and state income taxes. Some tax protections are available to those with military disability retirements, as discussed later in this chapter.

VA Disability Compensation: Reserve-component retirees with medical problems related to their military service can apply for VA Disability Compensation under the same rules that govern other veterans. See the section later in this chapter for full rules on the VA program.

A typical military retirement is also known as nondisability retirement, to distinguish it from the military's disability retirement program.

FIFTEEN-YEAR RETIRED PAY

Some reservists and National Guard members can qualify for retired pay after serving only fifteen years. The program is officially known as the Temporary Early Retirement Authority (TERA). In this case, "temporary" refers to the military's authority to approve these early retirements. Once an individual receives a TERA or fifteen-year retirement, it's guaranteed for life.

Eligibility: Fifteen-year military retirements aren't a right. They're a tool used by personnel planners to give the military the proper mix of skills and ranks and to help reserve-component members whose units close or move.

Eligible people must have at least fifteen "good" or "creditable" years, but less than twenty years. A "good" year is usually a twelve-month period during which a reservist or guard member earns at least fifty points through active-duty service, attendance at weekend drill periods, annual active-duty training, or other active-duty or inactive-duty training.

Fifteen-year retirees, like their more traditional counterparts, must wait until their sixtieth birthdays to begin collecting retired pay.

Rates: The same formula is used that's discussed in the rates section under "Typical Retired Pay," earlier in this chapter.

COLAs: Like the more typical twenty-year military retirees, fifteen-year retirees have periodic—usually, annual—

increases in their retired pay known as cost-of-living adjustments.

Other Benefits: Recipients of fifteen-year retirements are entitled to the same retired benefits as twenty-year retirees and recipients covered by the military's disability retirement program. These include medical care and lifelong access to such on-base facilities as commissaries and exchanges.

INCAPACITATION PAY

Many of the financial protections for injured military people were written for the active-duty force, then adapted for the reserve components. One program, however, was created by the government with reservists and National Guard members in mind. It's called Incapacitation Pay, and it can be used when none of the government's other financial protections seem to fit.

Eligibility: Qualification depends on certain factors affecting both the reservist and the medical problem.

When the disability begins recipients must be members of the reserves or National Guard:

- On active duty for thirty days or less,
- On inactive duty, or
- Traveling directly to or from inactive or active duty lasting thirty days or less.

> Incapacitation Pay may be paid because a person can't do his military or civilian job.

Specifically not eligible, under federal law, are reservists hurt during correspondence courses or while officially classified as being on inactive status to attend an educational program sponsored by one of the armed forces.

The medical problem for which Incapacitation Pay is sought must be an injury, illness, or disease that was caused or aggravated when the reservist was in one of the three eligibility periods mentioned above. That medical problem must affect the reservist's ability to perform either military duties or a civilian job.

Rates: The amount of Incapacitation Pay is calculated according to a two-step process.

It begins with the Basic Pay, BAQ, and BAS that the servicemember would receive on active duty. From that figure is subtracted any other income, including benefits offered by a civilian employer, such as:

- Sick leave
- Vacation pay
- Payments from an income-protection plan

Some people receiving Incapacitation Pay are unable to hold down their military jobs, but are able to work at their regular civilian jobs.

For those people, the rules for Incapacitation Pay undergo another adjustment. The amount of Incapacitation Pay is reduced to fill any gap between what they made in their civilian jobs before the injury and what they're able to earn afterwards.

Under no circumstances can Incapacitation Pay exceed the amount of Basic Pay, BAQ, and BAS that a reservist or National Guard member would receive on active duty.

When recipients recover or their income exceeds minimal levels, Incapacitation Pay ends. It ends for everyone after six months. People still in need of financial assistance because of their injuries after six months can seek VA Disability Compensation, which is discussed later in this chapter.

TEMPORARY DISABILITY RETIREMENTS

When the government is unsure whether a reservist or guard member will be able to return to duty after having medical problems, the services have the option of putting that person on the Temporary Disability Retirement List (TDRL) until the situation is clarified. People receiving money under this program are said to be on the TDRL.

Eligibility: The TDRL was designed for people on full-time active duty. Reservists and guardsmen on shorter periods of active duty and on inactive duty can qualify, but only after a high-level, case-by-case review. Usually, reserve-component members on active duty for less than thirty days or on inactive duty would be given Incapacitation Pay instead of being put on the TDRL.

Participants must have health problems that may not be permanently disabling or, if permanent, have a degree of disability that is uncertain.

Physical Evaluation Boards examine the records of military personnel and decide who is placed on the TDRL. Military personnel have a right to present their cases to such boards. They can argue to go on the TDRL, to be discharged, or to return to active duty.

People on the TDRL are officially considered military retirees. They have no official duties, they are ineligible to live on base, and they lose eligibility for any military payments except TDRL money.

TDRL compensation cannot be combined with VA Disability Compensation. TDRL retirees who accept VA money are discharged.

Rates: There are two formulas that can be used to compute pay for those on the TDRL. They can choose the most generous formula:

- Multiply the last monthly Basic Pay by the percentage of disability assigned by a Physical Evaluation Board.
- Multiply the last monthly Basic Pay by twelve, and then multiply that figure by 2.5 percent for each year on active duty. Take that number and divide by twelve, yielding a monthly rate.

Whatever formula is used, personnel on the TDRL are

guaranteed a minimum of 50 percent of their Basic Pay, but they cannot receive more than 75 percent of Basic Pay.

Although some of the special pays related to hazardous duty have provisions allowing payment for hospitalized personnel, people on the TDRL are retired. Retirees are ineligible for money for hazardous duty.

Duration: As soon as the medical condition of those on the TDRL stabilizes, they are reevaluated, and then are either returned to military duty or discharged.

People discharged with lingering medical problems are given Disability Severance Pay, Military Disability Retirement Pay or VA Disability Compensation. The last two programs are discussed later in this chapter.

The longest anyone can stay on the TDRL is five years. If a person's medical condition is still uncertain at that time, he is discharged.

Time spent on the TDRL counts toward promotions and time in service for pay purposes, but it doesn't count toward regular length-of-service retirements.

MILITARY DISABILITY RETIREMENT

Most veterans whose health was impaired by military service find that the best protection for their financial needs is VA Disability Compensation, discussed later in this chapter. A smaller number of injured and ill veterans find that their needs are best met by Military Disability Pay. It's classified as a retired pay, and recipients are considered military retirees.

> A dollar of military *disability* pay must be waived for each dollar of VA Disability Compensation received.

Eligibility: All military members—active duty and reserve component—can receive a disability retirement from the armed forces if they are unable to perform their official duties because of health problems.

Most recipients have disabilities that are rated as being at least 30 percent, using the medical standards of the Department of Veterans Affairs.

Additionally, active-duty members, reserve-component members on extended active duty, and reserve-component members on active duty for periods of at least thirty-one days must have at least eight years in uniform—eight "good" years—or disabilities that were directly related to official duties, to wartime conditions, or to a national emergency.

Reserve-component members on active duty for thirty days or less or on inactive duty (as weekend drill periods are called) must have medical problems that meet the 30 percent threshold. Additionally, the medical problems must be directly related to military duties or to traveling to or from official duties (including the training site for a drill period).

Rates: In most instances, there are two formulas that can be used to compute the size of a veteran's Military Disability Retired Pay. The servicemember gets to use the more generous formula. The formulas are:

- Multiply the servicemember's monthly Basic Pay by the percentage of the disability
- Multiply the servicemember's monthly Basic Pay by 2.5 percent for each year on active duty

Basic Pay is the rate for the last month on active duty for those who first joined the military before September 8, 1980. For those who joined more recently, the Basic Pay figure that's used is the monthly average for the thirty-six months of highest Basic Pay.

Applications: Veterans can apply for a military disability retirement at any time, even years after they've left active duty.

However, the chances of qualifying are remote. Remember, this is a benefit paid to those who are unable to perform their military duties. If someone was showing up for work in the military, it's tough to prove years later that a medical condition prevented that person from doing the job.

Changes: The disability percentage assigned to a recipient of Military Disability Retired Pay never changes, even if the medical condition worsens. If a person's health deteriorates, the military expects the servicemembers to seek VA disability compensation, as discussed later in this chapter.

Other benefits: Recipients of Military Disability Retired Pay are military retirees, just like their length-of-service counterparts. They are eligible for commissary and exchange privileges and carry military ID cards. They can be treated in military medical facilities, although they're subject to the same access problems as other military retirees.

Retirees: People who already qualify for regular length-of-service retirement because they have at least twenty years in uniform can choose to have part of their retired pay consist of disability retired pay. The amount is the same percentage as the disability.

For example, someone retiring with twenty years' service with a 40 percent disability can have 40 percent of the retired pay classified as Military Disability Retired Pay. Twenty-year military retirees are eligible for Military Disability Retired Pay even if the medical problem is rated as less than a 30 percent disability.

Length-of-service retirees who receive some of their monthly checks as Military Disability Retired Pay must use the formula that relies on the disability percentage to compute the amount of Military Disability Retired Pay.

Taxes: The general rule on Military Disability Retired Pay is that it's taxed (see Chapter 6 for the exceptions).

VA Disability Compensation: Recipients of Military Disability Retired Pay must give up one dollar of that money for each dollar they receive in VA Disability Compensation, which is discussed below.

As a practical matter, most disabled military retirees discover that they can receive more from the VA's system than from the military's. An additional advantage is that the VA money is always tax free, whereas only some Military Disability Retired Pay is shielded from taxes.

VA DISABILITY COMPENSATION

Most veterans receiving money from the government for service-related medical problems actually receive checks from the Department of Veterans Affairs, not from the Department of Defense.

These payments are called VA Disability Compensation. Recipients aren't classified as military retirees unless they qualify for one of the military retirement programs discussed earlier.

Eligibility: Disability compensation can be paid to anyone who served in the military, including members of the reserves and National Guard, on various kinds of active duty and during inactive-duty periods (commonly called drill periods).

There is no minimum time that a person must spend in uniform to qualify.

Two major groups of veterans are *ineligible:*

• Veterans with discharges officially rated as "under dishonorable conditions"

• Veterans with disabilities caused by "willful misconduct," such as those incurred during commission of a crime, during unauthorized absences, or through the abuse of drugs or alcohol

> VA Disability Compensation may affect money paid to reserve-component members by the military.

The disability can be the result of an accident, injury, or illness. It could have arisen during military service, or it could have been aggravated by military service.

To be eligible, a veteran must prove—usually through military medical records—that the disability began (or was aggravated) between the first day in uniform and the last.

As a practical matter, most payments based on medical problems connected with inactive-duty status deal with injuries. It's tough to prove that a debilitating illness was acquired during a drill period rather than during the same day while the servicemember was at home.

Rates: VA Disability Compensation is a monthly payment made directly to a qualified veteran. The rates are based on the percentage of disability. That percentage, in turn, is based on a medical evaluation of the severity of a veteran's impairment.

Percentages are always divisible by ten. The amount of money assigned to each percentage usually changes every year to keep pace with inflation.

Veterans can apply for a change in the percentage assigned to their disability if it worsens over the years. They're not locked into one percentage for life.

VA Disability Compensation is always tax free. That includes federal, state, local, Social Security, and Medicare taxes.

Other Benefits: The monthly check for VA Disability Compensation isn't the most important benefit that most recipients get. They also receive free lifelong medical care in VA hospitals and clinics for their disabilities.

Here, a crucial distinction arises. People with disabilities rated 40 percent or lower can be treated only for the disability.

VA DISABILITY COMPENSATION RATES (1997)

Disability	*Amount*
10 %	$ 94
20	179
30	274
40	391
50	558
60	703
70	887
80	1,028
90	1,157
100	1,924

People with disabilities rated at 50 percent or higher can be treated, free of charge, for anything in a VA hospital or clinic.

Also available to veterans receiving VA Disability Compensation are:

- Vocational rehabilitation
- Dependents allowance (if the disability is rated 30 percent or higher)
- Financial help to take care of a spouse who needs assistance with daily tasks (also limited to veterans with disabilities rated 30 percent or higher)

Veterans with 100 percent VA disabilities may be eligible for some benefits from the military. They may be able to use commissaries and base exchanges and on-base recreational facilities, as can their spouses and dependent children. However, they are ineligible for military health care.

Also going to 100 percent disabled veterans is a reduced-cost health insurance program for spouses and dependent children. It's called CHAMPVA, or the Civilian Health and Medical

Program of the VA. It shouldn't be confused with the military's CHAMPUS health insurance program. Details about CHAMPVA are available from any VA office.

Military Retirees: VA Disability Compensation can be paid to military retirees. That includes people who qualify for the military's regular length-of-service retirement or for Military Disability Retired Pay.

For each dollar of VA money received, however, a military retiree must give up one dollar of military money. Most military retirees decide that it makes sense to surrender part of their retired pay, since VA Disability Compensation is always tax-exempt.

24

SPOUSES, EX-SPOUSES, AND SURVIVORS

In This Chapter:

- *Spouses*
- *Ex-Spouses*
- *Survivors*
- *Survivors of Retirees*

People wearing uniforms aren't the only ones who have a stake in the military compensation system or veterans' programs. Spouses, ex-spouses, survivors, and even the children of reserve-component members have some rights regarding military paychecks.

This chapter explores some of the financial programs and financial rights of the family members of military personnel. This is a summary, not a comprehensive listing. Anyone making important financial decisions should get help from a military lawyer, family support center, or other expert.

SPOUSES

The spouses of reservists and National Guard members have few direct rights to the military member's paycheck, but they do have some. They also should be aware of some procedures and rules.

Military Paycheck: Reservists and National Guard members on extended active duty can designate a spouse or a child to receive monthly payments directly from a military finance center. These payments, called allotments, are deducted from the military member's monthly pay.

The general rule is that reserve-component members are usually ineligible to create allotments based on Drill Pay, other inactive-duty pays, or active-duty income from short periods of full-time service.

Reservists and guard members become eligible to make allotments if they are brought on active duty for a national emergency or for periods lasting at least 180 days. People qualifying under the 180-day rule can make allotments from their first day on active duty; they don't have to wait 180 days to start.

Spouses—whether of active-duty people, reservists on active duty, or reserve-component people performing weekend drills—are limited in their ability to initiate allotments themselves, to change the amount of allotments, or to receive other direct payments from the military.

> It's nearly impossible for spouses to start, stop, or change allotments.

Note that several types of military pay, especially the housing allowances—BAQ, OHA, and VHA—have separate rates for people with dependents and those without dependents.

Anyone who claims those payments at the with-dependents rate when the dependents aren't being financially supported is receiving that extra money fraudulently. That's a serious charge, and the military will take it seriously.

Missing Status: When military members become prisoners of war, are missing in action, or are put on missing status, they continue receiving their regular pay and allowances.

They can earn promotions, accrue leave, and get pay raises. Any allotments to spouses that were in effect before they were missing continue. Each service has rules governing a spouse's ability to change those allotments.

Mental Incompetence: Family members may need a court order designating them as guardians or trustees for a mentally incompetent servicemember to gain access to that person's full military pay.

Until a court-appointed guardian has been named, the Army and Air Force designate the adjutant general as the trustee of the military member's pay. The Navy and Marine Corps name the finance center as the trustee.

EX-SPOUSES

Even for members of the reserve components, it's often difficult to separate personal concerns from professional issues. Perhaps for that reason, the military offers some protections to the former spouses of active-duty personnel.

Military Paycheck: When a court orders someone in uniform to provide financial support for an ex-spouse or children, the military can send part of the military member's pay directly to the ex-spouse or dependent children, without obtaining the member's permission.

This includes reservists and National Guard members on extended active duty and on shorter stints of active duty. It even includes Drill Pay and other income from inactive-duty status.

Ex-spouses can go to the Defense Finance and Accounting Service Center with a court order after servicemembers have fallen two months behind in child support or spousal support agreements. State agencies that deal with so-called deadbeat parents can file on the ex-spouse's behalf.

Servicemembers are supposed to be notified before any action is taken by the finance center on such a claim. They have the right to review copies of the documentation provided by the ex-spouse. They also have a chance to file their own documentation with the finance center.

This isn't a chance to reargue the divorce. Unless the servicemember can show that the payments have already been made or that the court order is erroneous, the finance center will honor the court order.

The finance center can send the ex-spouse:

• Up to 50 percent of the servicemember's disposable income if the servicemember has remarried or supports a dependent child.

• Up to 60 percent of the servicemember's disposable income if the servicemember hasn't remarried and hasn't acquired a dependent child.

• An additional penalty of 5 percent of the servicemember's disposable income if that person is at least twelve weeks behind in payments.

What's disposable income? It's determined by a two-step process. First, add together the servicemember's military income.

Second, subtract a few specific expenses:

• Debts and fines to the federal government
• Contributions to the Armed Forces Retirement Home
• Federal and state income taxes
• Premiums for Servicemember's Group Life Insurance

What's left is disposable income.

For reserve-component members on inactive-duty status—that is, for those collecting Drill Pay or performing comparable training—ex-spouses are limited to collecting the same percentages of military income that finance centers can send to the ex-spouses of active-duty people.

Moving: When servicemembers and their spouses break up during a stateside assignment, the military has no obligation to help the spouse and dependent children move out of the military member's home.

However, when the breakup occurs overseas, the military treats the move of the civilian spouse and dependent children as a permanent-change-of-station (PCS) move. The government pays to get people from one place to another and ships personal property, including one personal car.

One piece of fine print is very important for reserve-component families. To qualify, the spouse and children must be officially "command-sponsored" at the overseas location. Usually, that rules out everyone but the families of reservists and National Guard members on extended active duty.

Retirees: All military retirees can instruct a military finance center to subtract a portion of money from their retired pay and send it directly to an ex-spouse or child for alimony, child support, or a property settlement.

If a military retiree fails to abide by a court order for alimony, child support, or a property settlement, the ex-spouse can send the finance center a copy of the court order and request a direct payment.

For money owed to an ex-spouse as a property settlement, there are some preconditions before the finance center will send money directly to the ex-spouse:

- The marriage must have lasted at least ten years.
- At least ten years of the marriage must have been during what the military considers "creditable" or "good" years for retirement purposes.

This ten-year rule applies only to property settlements. Courts don't face any length-of-marriage restrictions when it comes to ordering direct payments from retired pay for alimony and child support.

Other government-paid benefits are due to three specific groups of ex-spouses. The definitions of these benefits are tough to understand, but it's necessary to spell out the exact limits of each group:

Free medical care for one year: To be eligible, the ex-spouse must have been married at least twenty years to a military member who spent at least twenty years on active duty; at least fifteen years of the marriage must have been during "creditable" military service; and the divorce must be completed after April 1, 1985.

Free medical care for life: To be eligible, the ex-spouse must have been married at least twenty years to a military member who spent at least twenty years on active duty; at least fifteen years of the marriage must have been during creditable military service; and the divorce must have been completed before April 1, 1985.

Free medical care for life, plus commissary and exchange access: To be eligible, the ex-spouse must have been married at least twenty years to a military member who spent at least twenty years on active duty, and at least twenty years of the marriage must have been during creditable military service.

Usually, the most that a finance center can send under a court order is 50 percent of a retiree's disposable income. That figure can rise to 65 percent when delinquent child support and alimony are included.

Disposable income includes retired pay the retiree declines to accept or waives in order to receive VA Disability Compensation. It does not include premiums paid for the Survivor Benefit Plan or federal and state income taxes.

SURVIVORS

When people die while in the military—including reservists and National Guard members during weekend drill periods and summer camps—their spouses and children are eligible for a variety of programs and payments from the federal government. The most important benefit is called Dependency and Indemnity Compensation (DIC).

Eligibility: DIC has two sets of eligibility rules, one for the military member and the other for survivors.

The military member must have:

• Died from a disease or injury that began during—or was aggravated by—active duty or active duty for training.

• Died from an injury that began during—or was aggravated by—inactive duty for training.

• Died from an injury that happened while the reservist or National Guard member was traveling from home to inactive duty or traveling from inactive duty back home.

• Died after discharge from the military—either active duty or as a reserve-component member—as a result of health problems caused or aggravated by active-duty service, active duty for training, or inactive duty for training.

> Most DIC recipients receive the same monthly payment. An earlier rank-based system ended for survivors in 1993.

Note that active-duty deaths can qualify family members for DIC if the deaths were caused by either injury or illness. Inactive-duty deaths and deaths on the road traveling to inactive duty must be related to injuries.

To qualify, a spouse must have:

• Been married for at least one year, if childless.

• Been married for any duration, with children.

• Been living continuously with the servicemember since marriage (except for separations through no fault of the spouse).

• Not remarried.

Children must fall into one of these categories:

• Have not reached their eighteenth birthday

• Have not reached their twenty-third birthday and are full-time students in an approved course of study

• Are older than eighteen and incapable of self-support because of physical or mental disability that began before the eighteenth birthday

Ineligible for DIC are the survivors of people who had at least twenty years of military service when they died on active duty. Those people are protected financially by the Survivor Benefit Plan (SBP), discussed later in this chapter.

Also ineligible are the survivors of reserve-component members whose deaths aren't linked to their military service or who receive payments under the SBP, as discussed later in this chapter.

Rates: Spouses who qualify for DIC receive the same monthly payment. In 1997, it was $833 a month. Generally, the rate increases annually to keep up with inflation.

Spouses of servicemembers and veterans who died before January 1, 1993, are covered by a different rate structure that is based on the rank of the military person.

The spouse's monthly DIC can be increased by several factors, listed below with the monthly 1997 rates for these conditions:

• For each child younger than eighteen—$211

• Surviving spouse who is housebound—$102

• Surviving spouse who is blind, in a nursing home, or in need of home care—$211

When there is no surviving spouse or when the surviving spouse is ineligible for DIC, the following monthly rates (1997) are paid to eligible children of the servicemember:

• One child—$354

• Two children—$510

• Three children—$662

• Each additional child after the third—$130

These monthly payments to eligible children can be increased under certain situations:

• Disabled child over age eighteen (spouse ineligible for DIC)—$211

- Disabled child over age eighteen (spouse gets DIC)—$354
- Child aged eighteen to twenty-three and in school—$179

DIC rates are unaffected by other sources of income or Social Security payments. Nor do DIC payments affect Social Security payments.

Technically, recipients of money under the SBP can also collect DIC, as long as they and their military spouses meet all the eligibility rules. But they lose one dollar of SBP money for each dollar of DIC.

SURVIVORS OF RETIREES

Retired paychecks stop after the death of a veteran. The Survivor Benefit Plan (SBP) is a government-backed program to ensure that the wives and husbands of deceased military retirees will have an income if they are left alone.

Eligibility: SBP has two sets of eligibility rules, one for the military member and the other for survivors.

The reservist or National Guard member must be officially credited with having twenty "creditable" or "good" years. These reserve-component members can provide SBP coverage to their spouses even if they continue to serve in the reserves or National Guard.

Separate eligibility rules apply to spouses and children. To qualify, a spouse must have:

- Been married for at least one year, if childless.
- Been married for any duration, with children.

Spouses who remarry before their fifty-fifth birthdays lose eligibility for SBP payments. Eligibility is restored if those new marriages end. Spouses who remarry after their fifty-fifth birthdays can continue receiving SBP payments.

The children of eligible veterans can qualify for SBP coverage. They can be protected along with their surviving parent, or they can be covered separately. To be eligible, children must fall into one of these categories:

- Have not reached their eighteenth birthday
- Have not reached their twenty-second birthday and are full-time students in an approved course of study
- Are older than eighteen and incapable of self-support because of a physical or mental disability that began before the eighteenth birthday

Also eligible to receive SBP payments are former spouses and dependent children of those marriages. If a former spouse is a servicemember's SBP beneficiary, the current spouse and dependent children from the current marriage are ineligible.

> Retired pay ends with a retiree's death. SBP is financial protection for survivors.

A final category of eligible SBP beneficiaries are those who have a provable financial interest in the survival of a retired reserve-component member. This may include business partners as well as family members who are financially dependent on the retiree, including parents, grandparents, grandchildren, aunts and uncles, brothers and sisters, half siblings, and stepchildren.

Application: The SBP requires people to make choices. Here are some of those decisions:

- After accumulating twenty years of military service, both on active duty and in the reserve component, the servicemember must decide within ninety days of being notified by the government that the twenty-year mark has been reached whether to take part in the SBP.
- If the decision is made to participate in the SBP at the twenty-year milestone, the servicemember must decide whether to provide survivors with SBP income immediately after the servicemember dies or to have payments start on what would have been the dead servicemember's sixtieth birthday.
- At the servicemember's sixtieth birthday, if the servicemember chooses not to participate in the SBP at the twenty-

year mark, the new retiree has ninety days to decide whether to participate.

• Whenever a reserve-component member decides to obtain SBP coverage for survivors, the reservist or guard member must also decide how much income to provide for a spouse, former spouse, or dependent child. A formula discussed below is used in that decision.

In theory, retirees can notify the government of these decisions in letters. But to prevent misunderstandings, people should use DD Form 1883, *Survivor Benefit Plan Election Certificate,* or DD Form 1882, *Survivor Benefit Plan Election Change.* The forms are available from any military personnel unit, military personnel office, or retiree affairs office.

If a military member decides at age sixty not to provide a spouse with full SBP coverage, the spouse must agree to that in writing. If there is no written agreement, the military automatically signs up the retiree for the maximum rate.

If retirees don't choose SBP coverage, their spouses receive no money from the military when the retirees die. Also getting no military income are the spouses of reservists and guardsmen who decided at the twenty-year mark not to take part in the SBP and who died before getting a second sign-up chance at their sixtieth birthday.

The general rule is that those who accept SBP coverage cannot drop out at a later date, and those who decide not to participate can't sign up at a later date.

There are exceptions, however. Retirees can drop out of the SBP if their spouses or dependent children die, if they divorce, or if they become permanently disabled.

Reserve-component retirees who previously declined to take part in the SBP can join after age sixty if they marry or acquire a new dependent child by birth or adoption.

Payments: How much a survivor receives under the SBP is determined by the amount of the military retiree's retired pay and by certain decisions the retiree makes.

The most that a survivor can receive is 55 percent of the servicemember's retired pay. Retirees can choose lesser amounts of coverage.

The first step in calculating SBP coverage comes when the retirees select a base, which is a portion of retired pay. Whatever the base, the survivor will get 55 percent of it.

For example, retirees getting $1,000 a month in retired pay who select the full amount as the base ensure that their survivors will get $550 in monthly SBP. If the retiree decides that the base is $400, the survivor will get 55 percent of it, which is $220.

SBP payments to survivors increase yearly to keep up with inflation. The amount of the increase is usually the same as the cost-of-living adjustment (COLA) going to military retirees, Social Security recipients, and veterans.

SBP payments are fully taxed under federal income tax law.

Some survivors may qualify for both SBP and DIC, which was discussed earlier in this chapter. They lose one dollar of SBP for each dollar of DIC that they receive.

SBP payments are reduced, in most cases, from 55 percent of the base to 35 percent once a survivor reaches age sixty-two and becomes eligible for Social Security.

Why does Social Security have an impact on SBP payments? Because in both programs, taxpayers pay for the majority of benefits. The average individual receives more in SBP and Social Security than he paid in premiums or taxes.

It's possible for retirees to ensure that their survivors aren't affected by this Social Security-related reduction. They can purchase what's known as SBP Supplemental Insurance at the same time they sign up for SBP coverage. That protection is paid through reductions to retired pay in addition to the usual SBP reductions.

Information about SBP supplemental insurance is available from on-base military retiree offices or the offices administering retiree payments.

Costs: For reserve-component retirees, the process of determining SBP costs relies on one of two formulas:

- 6.5 percent of the base
- 2.5 percent of the first $425 in the base, plus 10 percent of the amount in the base greater than $425

The $425 figure is an approximation for the late 1990s. In January 1996, it was $411. It increases each year by inflation, as measured by COLA increases.

The government automatically uses whichever of these two formulas is advantageous to the reserve-component retiree to determine SBP costs.

This figure is increased using charts too large and complicated to reproduce here that take into account:

- The retiree's age when choosing SBP coverage
- The age difference between the retiree and the spouse
- Whether the retiree is also covering dependent children
- Whether the retiree wants payments to begin immediately after death or on what would have been the retiree's sixtieth birthday

These factors typically result in an additional withholding of $20 to $50 a month from a reserve-component member's retired paycheck.

These costs are paid by withholdings from retired pay, but one significant group of SBP participants doesn't have any retired pay. These are the reservists who decided when they reached the twenty-year mark in uniform to provide SBP coverage to their spouses or dependent children.

These so-called gray-area retirees pay for that coverage after the fact. Once they reach age sixty and begin receiving retired pay, their SBP withholdings are slightly larger than usual to make up for the years of unpaid coverage.

The spouses of these gray-area retirees who receive SBP payments even though their retirees never paid any SBP premiums get SBP payments that are slightly smaller than what they'd get using the common formulas.

Index

NOTES

NOTES